curriculum
as spaces

OMPLICATED
CONVERSATION

A Book Series of Curriculum Studies

William F. Pinar
General Editor

Volume 45

The Complicated Conversation series
is part of the Peter Lang Education list.
Every volume is peer reviewed and meets
the highest quality standards for content and production.

PETER LANG
New York • Bern • Frankfurt • Berlin
Brussels • Vienna • Oxford • Warsaw

DAVID M. CALLEJO PÉREZ,
DONNA ADAIR BREAULT, WILLIAM L. WHITE

curriculum
as spaces

AESTHETICS, COMMUNITY,
AND THE POLITICS OF PLACE

PETER LANG
New York • Bern • Frankfurt • Berlin
Brussels • Vienna • Oxford • Warsaw

Library of Congress Cataloging-in-Publication Data
Callejo-Pérez, David M.
Curriculum as spaces: aesthetics, community, and the politics of place /
David M. Callejo Pérez, Donna Adair Breault, William L. White.
pages cm. — (Complicated conversation: a book series of curriculum studies; v. 45)
Includes bibliographical references.
1. Curriculum planning—Social aspects.
2. Education—Curricula—Social aspects. 3. Place-based education.
I. Breault, Donna Adair. II. White, William L. III. Title.
LB2806.15.C28   375'.001—dc23   2014027214
ISBN 978-1-4331-2511-9 (hardcover)
ISBN 978-1-4331-2510-2 (paperback)
ISBN 978-1-4539-1431-1 (e-book)
ISSN 1534-2816

Bibliographic information published by **Die Deutsche Nationalbibliothek**.
Die Deutsche Nationalbibliothek lists this publication in the "Deutsche
Nationalbibliografie"; detailed bibliographic data are available
on the Internet at http://dnb.d-nb.de/.

The paper in this book meets the guidelines for permanence and durability
of the Committee on Production Guidelines for Book Longevity
of the Council of Library Resources.

TABLE OF CONTENTS

ACKNOWLEDGMENTS

What began as a conversation about urban education, spaces and communities at a hotel lobby became a year-long endeavor to discover who we were as individuals undertaking this approach to space and curriculum. In that year, we have relied on the ideas, patience, and support of many people who believed that our work would find a voice and audience within the academic public. David M. Callejo Pérez wishes to thank Peter Lang Publishing and their staff for their vision in seeing the value of our work. I would also like to thank William Pinar for welcoming our book into the Complicated Conversation Series. And of course, to two great co-authors, Donna and Bill, and their partnership in this book. I would also like to express gratitude to my mentor and friend, Stephen M. Fain, for his continued support and wisdom. Additionally, Donald Bachand at Saginaw Valley State University for his investment in conversations about this and many other topics. As in my life, this project has benefited and grown immeasurably from the understandings offered by my amazing wife, Emily Callejo, whose vision is on display in the cover, and two enchanting daughters, Icie and Annie, who remind me of my role and purpose. Last, as always, I thank my parents, Jose and Barbara, who encouraged and sacrificed for me to thrive.

I would like to thank my wonderful colleagues, William and David, with whom I have enjoyed the conversations and challenges regarding our thinking throughout this process. I am also thankful for my mentors, Deron Boyles, Dorothy Huenecke, who introduced me to Dewey and aesthetics as a graduate student years ago, and for Brad Stone, who asked a college sophomore to read Richard Sennett's work. It was while sitting in the Philip Weltner Library at Oglethorpe University and reading Sennett's work that I was first and deeply intrigued by notions of space. I am also thankful for my family. Rick's support has been felt across continents as he begins his Fulbright in Moldova, and Audrey and Niamh have graciously given Mommy space to finish whatever she has been doing at the computer. Thank you all, near and far, for the impact you've had in my work and my life.

During the journey that became this book, there were many fellow sojourners who not only accompanied me, but also provided feedback and the courage to continue. First, of course, are my fellow authors, David and Donna. From informal discussions about the nature of space, the rising tide of national curriculum that denies the importance of locality in education, and the importance of thinking critically about the educational environment, an idea was born and the book began to take shape. At each junction along the path, we shared our thoughts, encouraged discussion, and most importantly maintained not only progress toward a goal, but also friendships. I would also like to thank my spouse, Dr. Sarah Beth Hinderliter. Her work on communities and the evolving ways in which aesthetics, politics, and education, seen through the lens of Jacques Rancière's philosophy, was instrumental in conceptualizing and completing my sections of the *Communities as Spaces*. There is no doubt that the many conversations and the gentle ways in which Beth clarified complex ideas helped lead me toward a deeper and richer understanding of aesthetics and education. However, Beth was not only a comforting intellectual presence. She also helped me find the time and energy to work toward completion of the book as deadlines approached and multiple tasks loomed. And finally, I wish to thank Lennon, Sophie, and Zora. Each and every day, they remind me in many ways how beautiful life is.

We must learn to reawaken and keep ourselves awake, not by mechanical aids, but by an infinite expectation of the dawn, which does not forsake us even in our soundest sleep. I know of no more encouraging fact than the unquestionable ability of man to elevate his life by a conscious endeavour.

Henry David Thoreau

PROLOGUE—ORIGINS AND FOUNDATIONS

Curriculum as Spaces: Aesthetics, Community, and the Politics of Place (*Curriculum as Spaces*) is grounded in recent theoretical thinking on communities, cosmopolitanism, and aesthetics as they pertain to the field of education, broadly, and curriculum more specifically. Over the past several decades, a restrictive narrative that places assessment, accountability, and measurement at the fore have gained favor as the means to rectify the supposed deficiencies of education even as educational theorists have drawn attention to the need for pedagogies of place (Callejo Perez, Fain, & Slater, 2004), pedagogies that question the prevalence of "acquisitiveness" (Schubert, 2009), and the necessity of conversations that are challenging and complex rather than reductive (Pinar, 2001). We argue, in various ways and voices, that education is not a depoliticized act or theory that is of little consequence to communities and to people. Rather, in response to an increasing displacement of curriculum from the locality to the federal level, we propose an ecological design to curriculum in which education becomes more than rote memorization of isolated facts. More specifically, we seek to re-centered curriculum on the common experiences of communities and the individuals who inhabit them. Although not specifically addressed within this work, *Curriculum as Spaces* places John Dewey's naturalistic philosophy, in which he questions the static models of interaction that deny interconnectedness between organisms and the environment they inhabit, into dialog with the work of Jean-Luc Nancy (2001/2002) who imagined that communities are built upon a contingent being together that creates unity out of singularity.

The present work began simply enough as a series of informal conversations between friends. Sitting around conference and dinner tables at the American Association for Teaching and Curriculum's 2012 conference in San Antonio, Texas, we began to ponder the myriad of ways in which contemporary education has not only stripped meaning from schooling, but has also created anesthetic experiences for most learners. As we delved more deeply into questions of critical geography and educational ecology, we began to form the kernel of the idea for this book. Following Lisa Cary's (2006) call for curriculum spaces as epistemological concepts that emerge from historical, social, political, and economic dialogues; we set about the task of writing *Curriculum as Spaces*.

While each of us worked alone, we were cognizant of our overarching theme and the ways in which we wished to explore pedagogies of place. As a common frame, we chose Dewey's *Art as Experience* and his well-established tendency toward naturalistic philosophy. While honoring his work, we also moved into other philosophical traditions that speak clearly and cogently to place, communities, and interconnectedness. Among those, we explored either together or individually *Communities of Sense* (Hinderliter, Kaizen, Maimon, Mansoor, & McCormick, 2009), an edited volume that is built upon Jacques Rancière's questioning of the possibilities, potential, and the amorphous make up of communities, Michel Foucault's reflexive pedagogy as seen in his response to utopian ideals, and William Schubert's (2009) recent work that calls attention to the need for learner- and community-centered educational reform. From these works, and others, we began to see ways that schooling can recover the intimate relationship between curriculum and aesthetics. We began to deepen our conviction that place-based education, attending to the individual within community, is an avenue for educational reform that possesses the promise to re-awaken learners to education's latent emancipatory potential. We became, in short, excited about our conversation, complex and cacophonic at times, but nonetheless rewarding.

Unfolding the Narrative

As the narrative unfolded both within our writings and through our conversations, we discovered three interconnecting themes within our examination of the multiple spaces of curriculum. As concepts emerged and re-emerged just as a fine thread binding the fabric of the book, we realized that we had happened upon a multi-scalar approach to the topic that privileged complex conceptualizations of space, time, and engagement. More specifically, we explored the complicated notion of aesthetics as the potential to heighten sensitivity to the lived experiences and situated contexts of learners. Aesthetic education, in this recovered form, will neither be contingent upon art as a descendent from the lived form nor a path toward reconnecting the abstracted art to personal experience. Rather, aesthetic education is seen to be principally the raising of consciousness in defiance of numbing, or anesthetic educational experiences. These notions stem, in part, from Paulo Freire's *Pedagogy of the Oppressed*, but extend to the creation of a pedagogy of perception and feeling that relies on questions of place and space to privilege explication of lived experiences for critical thinking and self-reflection.

Within this vision of aesthetics, we saw the importance of community identity and the myriad of ways in which meaning-making and identity emerge from of the authentic transactional work needed to support growth. We need to ensure that the communities we achieve in schools and universities are cosmopolitan communities (Appiah, 2006; Greene, 2004; Hansen, 2010; Nussbaum, 1997/2009). We need to find ways in which we can balance the student as a "being half hidden in a cloud of unknowing" (Huebner, 1975, p. 219) with the larger social aims of a democratic society. This chapter addresses the conditions needed in order to achieve a cosmopolitan community in schools and universities. It outlines how the principles of cosmopolitanism support a transactional space for engaged meaning making and growth. Further, it examines the challenges in each context, and argues that social and pedagogical rituals provide means through which we can counteract these challenges. And finally, we re-think urban spaces and openly question the uniformity with which recovery, education, and social plans have been unilaterally imposed on large, yet infinitely diverse, cities. In so doing, we call attention to the fact that in an era of community change— specifically in the urban U.S.—it is crucial to understand the role of space and community development, revitalization, and identity on both the structures that make up the community and its people. Understanding what happens in public spaces is important if we are to respond to the challenges posed by this powerful concept. Casemore (2005) captures this feeling about landscapes— in his case in the rural South—that provide both psychological and historical impressions on individuals, which become a foundation for a personal lens. This section connects the intentional act of design and the concept of public space in a way that invites those who toil in the community to reconsider their positions on development and *the space of possibility* (Bourdieu, 1993).

As we completed the work, we held true to the overall point of view that a re-emergence of community in pedagogy and curriculum holds the potential to overcome the essentialist and reductive pedagogies of contemporary schooling. Yet, as in all complex conversations, divergent points of view emerged. Rather than submerge these under the goal of a common and intricately unified plan, we opted to allow voices to show themselves and to add the complexity of the task at hand, for indeed, curriculum is a complicated conversation that has no end and no easy answers. The road was long, but fruitful. We emerged on the other side with new ways of reflecting upon communities, aesthetics, and pedagogy. We maintained strong friendships. And, we hopefully added another voice to the long conversation that is, has been, and will always be curriculum.

Modernity, Education, and Control

Although neither educators nor politicians, Frederick Winslow Taylor's and Henry Ford's influence on American schooling is perhaps not well known but nonetheless undeniable. As a foreman in the Midvale Steel Works in Philadelphia, PA, Taylor developed an early approach to the study of efficiency, productivity, and predictability that became the foundations for "scientific management," whether in factories or schools (Moran, 2012). In a business-oriented quest to streamline manufacturing processes, *Taylorism*, as scientific management principles were often known, sought to simultaneously improve efficiency and profitability while also removing the risks associated with worker autonomy. While Taylor focused attention on management, Henry Ford "improved" production by re-inventing the assembly line within large factories (Dassbach, 1991). The general principles of "Fordism" were first enunciated by Karl Marx within his discussion of large-scale manufacturing processes and included the deconstruction of tasks, specialization of tools, and the creation machine systems that allowed uniformity in assembly lines and which has since been labeled *Fordism* (Beynon, 1973; Sabel, 1983). Originally intended as organizing and managerial principles for profit-oriented industries, *Taylorism* and *Fordism* quickly crept into many areas of society, including education. As rapid increases in population and school attendance took place in the late 19th and early 20th centuries, codification and control of procedures became vital to the regularization of procedures and the "democratic" promise of equality.

While it is relatively easy to see scientific management and production principles in early factory and social efficiency models of education, with specific interest in administrative structures (Tyack, 1974; Karier, 1975), the unfortunate truth is that this management model remains well-entrenched today. As assessment, standardization, performance objectives, and other such clinical terms proliferate, schools and schooling have become less concerned with individual student growth within the community than with organizational structures, cost analysis, and strict implementation of national standards.

In the current age of assessment, curriculum is formed on the principles of scientific management and has become a product, tangible and well-formed, that can be delivered by trained operators who are asked to think as little as possible as they complete their daily tasks. The risk of revolution, the challenges of change, and the inherent ambiguity of learning have vanished. Gone, as well, is the notion of curriculum as a complicated conversation (Pinar, 2008) that is situated within a context that brings together teacher, student, and text in the pursuit of individual as well as collective meaning-making. William Pinar (2008) perhaps sums the situation up best when noting that

> Instead of employing school knowledge to complicate our understandings of ourselves and the society in which we live, teachers are forced to 'instruct' students to mime others' (i.e., textbook authors) conversations, ensuring that countless classrooms are filled with ventriloquists rather than intellectual exploration, wonder, and awe (Pinar, 2008, p. 186).

As we approached the current work, we recognized, like Pinar (2008), that the deep connections between teaching, curriculum, and place have been torn asunder. Likewise, we noted that in an age of assessment and accountability and pervasive *Taylorism/Fordism*, pedagogy has been redefined as an interactional and largely instrumental act that resembles the Freirean Banking Model. With this as the background, we sought to add another voice to the complicated conversations that serve to reinvigorate the curriculum field even as top-down approaches to teacher education and schooling seem to sap energies and remove concern for social justice and reconstruction (Pinar, 2006). Yet, we realized that conversations are, at once, multi-layered, never-ending, and often difficult in a society where civic culture appears to reward exaggerated political positions and coarse public discourse (Rodin &

Steinberg, 2011). With this in mind, we have undertaken the complicated and critical task of presenting a work not of disengaged academics, but rather of public intellectuals who argue for educational significance (Pinar, 2004; 2006; Tierney & Lincoln, 1997) while simultaneously reaffirming the connections between curriculum, pedagogy, and place. Our work is therefore unabashedly political and meant to suggest the continued need, among all educators, for open conversations about what is possible, not what is prescribed.

Place, Space, and Communities

Curriculum as Spaces can be viewed as a holistic approach to education, conservation, and community development that uses the place as an integrating context for learning. As the name suggests, we recognize the multiplicity and idiosyncratic nature of spaces even within seemingly homogenous contexts. This follows, of course, the work of Maxine Greene (2001) that emphasize the seemingly contradictory but ultimately connected significance of solitude to dialogical processes and John Dewey's (1896) naturalism that saw intimate connections between individuals and the environments of which they were a part. *Curriculum as Spaces* seeks, therefore, to foster a partnership between people and communities and pedagogies and curriculum.

In this book we argue that curriculum and place have deep connections that are rooted in aesthetics, community, politics, and transactional pedagogies. Mirroring works by Pinar (2004/2008), Robert Lake (2010), and William Reynolds (2013) that strive to reconnect meaning to place, we attempt to go beyond the individual and address the profoundness of the concepts of space and place on the formation of belief systems. Many of these works, including *Curriculum as Spaces*, are informed by the personal and place-based struggles of the civil rights movement. With good reason, much has been made of the seminal civil rights marches, sit-ins, and boycotts that captured the attention of the nation and which promoted, at significant cost, social change. Yet, beginning in the 1980s and early 21st century, scholars such as Clayborne Carson (1986), Emma Lapsansky-Werner, Gary Nash (Carson, Lapsansky-Werner, & Nash, 2005), Steven Lawson (1991), and Charles Eagles (2000) began to reconsider the historiography of the civil rights movement to reflect a new awareness of the importance of locality (Dittmer, 1995). Within these efforts, no single institution stands taller than the southern black church. Whether embracing the revolutionary vigor and vision of Nat Turner or more reserved in their tone, black churches were the epicenter for changing attitudes about the place of blacks in America (Calhoun-Brown, 2000). Churches not only provided spiritual comfort and promise of a better day, they were social sites that provided a safe space and place for action and the setting for a complex social and educational curriculum infused with art, politics, education, and social services (Calhoun-Brown, 2000). The renewed emphasis on the role of individual churches in larger movements informs the question of pedagogies of place, of localized curricula, that attend to the social and educational needs of individuals within communities.

Although church leaders engaged the numerous social ills that plagued the south, there was none more pernicious and dangerous than the lack of educational opportunities for blacks of all ages. By the early 1960s, the notion of curriculum as space was well entrenched in the south and became a vital element in the foundation of educational programs, including the Head Start in Mt. Beulah, Mississippi. Alongside this recognized social change, informal groups used place to drive social change in traditional institutions (black and white) that had been created to maintain and cope with segregation. Freedom Schools in the South, civil rights workers and their organizations, and urban workers redefined the idea of curriculum as space.

In cities across the United States, urban plight and poverty led the cities to allow schools to be run by local school boards (Brownsville), focus on local populations, and allow alternative school within school buildings. Examples, such as Central Park East (founded by Deborah Meier), reinvigorated curriculum as space in schools. In Berkeley, Chicano studies emerged as a high school major; and the Black Panthers began running community schools in Oakland. In Texas and Louisiana, ethnic groups (Vietnamese and Mexican) founded language schools. In 1963, Coral Way Elementary (Miami-Dade, Florida, County Public Schools) became the first bilingual school (educating children in the day and parents at night). These examples of place driving curriculum evolved from the same philosophy of access to education for all persons who live within communities and representations of their identity. However, in the 1970s, society and more specifically, schooling, became less focused on place and more on a de facto national culture dominated by what Neil Postman (1995) and Michael Apple (1996) both defined as technological oligarchy. During this time, economic crises, pollution, urban blight, rural poverty, and the widening gulf among the wealthy and poor. Additionally, Hispanic migration led communities to rethink ideas of place and identity. This led many to turn to a system of place-based education as a solution to the outliers within the normalcy of cultural identity. What occurred was that place-based became synonymous with place and space—which it is not. The writing on this topic interchanges place-based with space and place. Recent arguments by authors that use Kincheloe's (1991) writings on philosophy of identity through literature and a previous work by one of the authors (Callejo et al., 2004) that sought to explore how to rethink pedagogy through place have been broadly cited as arguments for place-based education and/or creating space, rather than examining the deeper interaction between the psychological and physical in its historical wholeness such as the relationship between literature, race, and slavery or art, gender, and political movements.

Even with these unique efforts to address the curriculum of space, major issues persist. The first is the rigor of curriculum studies is not applied to this complex field that encompasses philosophy, aesthetics, geography, social theory and history. Second is the conflict that studying the place without contextualizing within the larger social milieu misses nuances because today we are more intimately tied to a global social network than to a regional one. Third is the uncritical assessment of underrepresented groups within the theoretical landscape—ignoring. Children of color or diverse ethnicities, religions, or exceptionalities find themselves not included. Ironically, the national curriculum (federal law) has borne the onus for curricular inclusion. Fourth is how to define the role of non-school organizations such as community action groups, hospitals, clinics, 4-H, Future Farmers of America, Rotary Clubs, and University Extension within the local curriculum. Also, and more importantly in an era where all curriculum in K–12 schooling (and in higher education) must be measured or assessed, how do we measure the impact of learning when all programs are unique to place?

Place-based curricula have thematic patterns that include (1) cultural studies, (2) nature studies, (3) internships and entrepreneurial opportunities (a chance to think about local vocational options), and (4) sustainability (examples include the Foxfire project, run by the teachers and students in Georgia in the 1970s). In general, contemporary schooling in the United States has been reformed to respond to the imperatives of globalization and economic growth. Curriculum developers proposed an industrialized factory model or urban model as the models of public education in United States—and this model has dominated not only 20th-century developments but continues to do so, thereby questioning the place of place-based curriculum.

Aesthetics and Re-awakening the Lived Connection to Education

Curriculum as Spaces reconsiders and attempts to complicate the meaning of aesthetics within education. While questions of aesthetics have long been a part of the educational landscape, until recently the word aesthetics was primarily associated with questions of beauty. And indeed, in many museums, art galleries, and other venues, we often still hear patrons whisper "that is aesthetically pleasing" or "the aesthetic qualities are well aligned in that work" when discussing the beauty of a piece of art. Nonetheless, theorists in many areas, including politics, geography, and increasing education have begun to expand the meaning of aesthetics to encompass the unity, interconnectedness, and emergent qualities of experiences. In so doing, they have created a neo-aesthetic movement that draws its relevance from ancient Greece, where aesthetics meant sense perception or the capacity to be a sentient being. In the chapters two and six, we attempt to connect educational practices to this neo-aesthetic stance in an effort to combat the anesthetic, or numbing experiences that are pervasive in many education settings. This requires, in short, a reconnection to pedagogies of place that promotes a re-awakening of lived experiences and which lead to aesthetic moments—those precise points of connectedness that are built on self-reflection and ambiguity.

As we discuss aesthetics and education, we recognize the significant contributions of John Dewey, Monroe Beardsley, Maxine Greene, and others. We are also aware of the long and shared histories of aesthetics and education. Indeed, in ancient Greece, Plato's concerns about the proper education, or perhaps more correctly, the appropriate content of an education began the linkages between questions of beauty and education. While rather prescriptive, the Platonic ideals followed the general theme of the connectedness of art and education to the daily life that had begun with the prehistoric creation of trinkets, shell beads, and cave art. In many ways, Platonic notions of art and philosophy remain present today, shaping theory and creating unbreakable linkages between artifacts and educational practice.

Following the Platonic ideal, Monroe Beardsley (1982), in *The Aesthetic Point of View*, offered one popular definition linking some type of performance or object to an aesthetic experience. While noting that the central point of aesthetic education is perfecting taste, he contended that a true aesthetic was an intentional binding of a mental activity to an object. Through concentration and intentionality, unity between thought and form yields pleasurable experiences that were inherently beautiful and disinterested. Yet, it is precisely these linkages between art and educational practice, or what might be called educational aesthetics, that we wish to question. An aesthetic experience is not dependent upon external objects. It is, quite to the contrary, shaped by self-reflection and self-awareness that is brought about by exploring personal narratives that are found in the common experiences of communities where individuals live, work, and create meaning.

Although we attempt to deterritorialize the connections between art and aesthetic experiences, we nonetheless find interesting and informative parallels between the pedagogical sites tied to education and art – that is schools and museums. As institutions of cultural transmission, museums and schools are equally responsible for institutionalizing the relationship between individuals and the meaning of the worlds they inhabit. Each, in their own way, separates phenomena into distinct categories. Each offers only glimpses of the wonderfully holistic worlds from which individual elements were plucked. Each operates in ways that flattens the landscape that it purports to explore.

As an analog to schools, museums offer an enticing metaphor for problems also found in education. Indeed, in the world of art, as patrons meander the corridors and exhibition halls of museums, they often marvel at the quality of the artwork and installations (the intricacy, beauty, and size) while also puzzling over the connections between the disparate pieces that hang on the walls or stand on the floors. Some might be aware of spatial relationships of closeness and/or distance. Others might remark on color schemes, while still others might notice relationships of historical periods. For many museum goers, the "noticing" of these often superficial relationships might be sufficient. Other visitors, however, might remain baffled by what appears to be a paucity of more meaningful connections between museum pieces, the community, and larger cultural currents. As we explore both art and education, the lack of connections and self-reflexive explorations seems to suggest a foundation question for collections, whether they be art- or knowledge-based. That is, in short, what reflexive and consequential relationship exists between individual pieces in museum and gallery collections, the audience, and larger social contexts? Superficially, the answer seems to be obviously one of beauty, or aesthetic qualities. And indeed, such well-known intellectuals as Immanuel Kant, Martin Heidegger, Jacques Derrida, John Dewey, and Theodor Adorno considered aesthetics from artistic, philosophical, political, and educational vantage points. Yet, Jay Bernstein (1992) suggests that each of these approaches to art (and education) constitutes a non-reflexive monologue in which the observer witnesses some "objective" Truth without the ability to participate in truth-making. Art, education, and by consequence notions of aesthetics have been divorced from both context and the phenomenological lived conditions of individuals and has resulted in a fundamental alteration, indeed alienation, of personal relationships with what is important, what is good, and what is meaningful.

With this in mind, we can return momentarily to the admittedly rhetorical question of the relationship between art and individuals. The answer seems tantalizingly close, but forever just beyond our touch. While Bernstein's focus on aesthetic alienation, or the separation of art and aesthetics from "truth," informs our discussion, the inability to lay our hands and minds upon the answer is perhaps best explained by Bourdieu's rather blunt and troublesome assessment of the effect of social capital, also read as power, upon aesthetic taste and artistic offerings (Bourdieu & Passeron, 1977). Galleries, museums, and school-based curricula are not about unified wholes that aim to explore reflexivity and relationships between knowledge, individual, and the larger community. Rather, they are often a series of un- or loosely related pieces that serve to "school" observers into acceptance of the taste of the refined and dominant socio-cultural class. Collections, in short, offer a catalog of artistic artifacts as well as a compendium of acceptable knowledge that serve to inculcate the less powerful in society in the norms and values of the powerful, thereby fueling a pervasive hegemony.

Museums and Education: A Metaphor. Art collections and educational curricula are therefore not unlike the almost mythological Palazzo Enciclopedico (The Encyclopedic Palace) of Marino Auriti. In November, 1955, Auriti, an Italian American artist, filed an architectural diagram with the U.S. Patent Office. Auriti's plan, for a 136-story building rising some 700 meters above the Washington, D.C. landscape, depicted his Palazzo Enciclopedico, a vast museum/library that would house the entirety of the world's knowledge. Although Auriti's plan was obviously never carried out, Massimiliano Gioni paid homage to the concept by adapting it as part of his curatorial plan for the 55th Venice Biennale (2013). Gioni, known for pairing serious purposes with humor (Goldstein, 2013), used Auriti's obsession with gathering and cataloging knowledge to question the canonization of art and artists by including lesser-known artist whose images and work possess depth, continuity, and longevity. Gioni moves away, in a sense, from the long-held notion of aesthetics as a question of cultivated and cultured taste to one that portends a precise moment, not of the past or present, but as a gateway to the dreams of the future that might or might not be fully developed. In so challenging the modern museum, or what Bernstein (1992) would call the hegemony of the modern, Gioni sought the possibility of exploring a world seen as a source of meaning beyond the normalizing effects of the modern aesthetic.

Gioni's understanding of the curatorial act, of gathering and disseminating knowledge, is well situated within contemporary and critical notions of collecting and can perhaps be seen as a direct descendent of Michel Thévoz's antimuseum that housed collections of Art Brut. The antimuseum, located in the west wing of the Château de Beaulieu, contained pieces that had been created by artists who worked within the freedom of anonymity and disinterest. Pascal-Désir Maisonneuve, Bill Traylor, and Madge Gill, among others, were outsider artists who had not been corrupted by "educational domestication" (Thévoz's term) and who resisted what Haacke (1983) called the museum's attempt to hone the sword of cultural reproduction and reification of certain works and socio-cultural beliefs. Not unlike Gioni's questioning of contemporary art practices, Thévoz profoundly tested the concept of contemporary museums by demonstrating that "non-professional artists provide evidence that all individuals are in fact potential creators" (Piery, 2001, p. 177).

Within education, an anti-schooling agenda, much like the antimuseum, would open learning to a broader array of experiences that are marked by commonalities within communities rather than adherence to anesthetic and DIS-placed curricula. While a trickle of important works, including William Pinar's (2004/2008) *What Is Curriculum Theory?*, Robert Lake's (2010), *Reconstructing Multicultural Education: Transcending the Essentialist/Relativist Dichotomy Through Personal Story*, and William Reynolds' edited volume (2013), *A Curriculum of Place: Understandings Emerging Through the Southern Mist*, have all spoken to what Pinar called "the nightmare of the present" and the silence of the public intellectual, more is needed. While the conversation is indeed complex and complicated, we hope to add our voices to the growing chorus calling for educational reform that focuses on pedagogies of place and human security.

In chapter two, we begin our discussion of aesthetics and the ways in which an aesthetic education complicates taken-for-granted attitudes, heightens learning, and mitigates the pernicious effects of rote and meaningless education by calling attention to the genealogical history of aesthetics. While admittedly truncated, the short history informs our understanding of the long connection between art and aesthetics. More importantly, however, the chapter wends its way toward conceptualizing aesthetics, within education, as the ability to perceive both present realities and future possibilities. As such, we see aesthetics as fundamentally concerned with the transformative potential that accompanies moments of questioning that portend emotional, social, and intellectual growth. Importantly, these moments are predicated on recognition of self within community that is closely aligned with a "partage du sensible," a concept developed by Jacques Rancière that plays on the double meaning of the French words "partager" and "sensible." On one hand "partager" means "splitting off" or "separating." On the other, it means "sharing." As for "sensible," we recognize both sense perceptions as well as recourse to intellect as possible meanings. When seen through the lens of pedagogies of place, we become aware that a "partage du sensible" requires individuals to situate educational possibilities within the spaces and places they occupy as well as the intellectual potential they possess.

In chapter six, we consider educational reforms, or what Pinar calls "deforms." from historical and contemporary perspectives. Emerging from the weight of a DIS-placed focus on national curricula and standards, we propose pedagogies of place that challenge contemporary schooling's insistence on "content mastery over critical thinking" as well as the strict adherence to time management that fails to recognized individual learner needs or the importance of play, curiosity, and exploration in education. We also call attention to the importance of accents in education and promote experiences that reverberate with the potential for a future replete with hope, joy, and fulfillment! All in all, we seek an aesthetic education built on experiences that awaken individuals to the challenges and possibilities in the worlds they inhabit. Likewise, we hope to draw attention to the failing one-size-fits-all educational system that de-emphasized human security (Means, 2014) while promoting an educational hegemony enmeshed in neo-liberal and neo-conservation agendas promoted by current and former presidential administrations.

Cosmopolitanism, Engagement, and Transactional Curriculum

As we considered the importance of community, engagement, and connections between individuals, we were naturally drawn to the question of cosmopolitanism and the ways in which it promotes living in healthy relationships with others. Just as Dewey (1938) suggested that individuals are not only affected by the environments in which they live, but in turn also affect their environment; so it is important to note the importance of authentic and bi-directional engagement within communities. We argue, in short, for an authentic re-engagement with curriculum and pedagogy that focuses not on the prescriptive and highly reductive standards currently in place, but rather on a multi-scalar curriculum reform that rejects linear trajectories while promoting multiplicities of experiences and meaning-making rituals.

The chapters (one and three) that focus on this theme are informed by William Hogarth's (1751) painting *Gin Lane*. Just as those portrayed in this painting seemingly meander through life without engaging their surroundings or their neighbors, we suggest that contemporary curriculum does much the same. Sanitized worksheets, timed assignments, and other examples of "best practices" often create more passivity among learners than engagement. We suggest that re-aligning curriculum with the spaces in which it resides can result in a fundamental change in schooling. That is, we can usher in an age of authentic transactional engagement that attends to the totality of the environment and which promotes lived-in connections.

In this view, curriculum and pedagogy are not static phenomena that exist but seemingly go unnoticed and certainly unattended to. Rather, they co-exist in equal partnership and are simply the tools that caring teachers use to approach and engage learners. We realize, however, that this view of curriculum and pedagogy is easily articulated yet hard to enact. Following Joseph Schwab (1969), we note the importance of language and self-critical stances. If we, as educators, continue to accept the outsourcing of the language of our profession to others, we risk continued marginalization. And, unfortunately, we become complicit in our own demise. We must not succumb to public pressure to use the language of accountability and assessment in our personal and professional narratives. We must, in short, reclaim the lost language of meaningful curricular reform.

We realized fully the difficulty of this task. As we respond to the stakeholders of our profession, the public, we appreciate that the very public nature of our profession works against meaningful reform initiatives. Indeed, while the general public has mostly been educated, having served 12 or more years in an educational prison, they are not truly cognizant of the unarticulated goals and processes on which public education is predicated. Further, as Dewey (1929) noted, humans are drawn to the certainty of measurement and the assurances that tests and evaluations prove ultimate worth. These experiences and beliefs often lead the public to believe that they know as much about education and what is needed to solves its

problems as educational professionals. Although we do not intend to alien-
ate the public, we nonetheless need to find ways, as public intellectuals, to
engage them in the complicated conversation that is curriculum—that is,
in fact, the future.

And finally, these chapters (one and three) remind us to be mindful of
the reductive arguments that swirl around educational reform. We note the
important political and moral obligation that we have to promote social
and individual justice with the communities and spaces we inhabit. We, in
short, put forth a call for action, a call for passion, and a call for authentic
re-engagement in the conversations that form curricula.

Conclusion

As we looked over the pages that follow, we noticed that neatly couched within calls for a retreat to community and place-based educational opportunities,
a thread of social and individual justice as well as the call for a more politi-
cized stance for education was infused throughout the chapters. This follows,
of course, William Pinar's two-decade-long (now three) discourse on collec-
tivity, individuality, and justice (Kincheloe, 1998). It also aligns with Cirenio
Rodriguez and Enrique Trueba's (1998) claim that political socialization, i.e.,
reinforcing attitudes and beliefs about place and possibilities, are present in
schooling and that only individuals who are well-aware of the conditions of
their communities can provide the leadership to overcome the "hegemonic
structures, poverty, oppression and ignorance" rampant in many localities
(p. 48).

As we conclude this introduction, we once again call attention to the
importance of community in education and the interconnectedness of individuals who live together in vibrant and nourishing communities, and, like
Paulo Freire (1995), question the origins of curriculum and note that for us
"the fundamental problem—a problem of a political nature—is who chooses
the content, and in behalf of which persons and things the "chooser's" teaching will be performed …in favor of whom, against whom, in favor of what,
against what" (Freire, 1995, p. 109).

THE TRANSACTIONAL SPACES
OF CURRICULUM

Rethinking "Community" and Re-Engaging Educators

In the past four decades, narratives regarding curriculum have shifted away from their original experiential core. Rather than focusing on the quality of a shared, lived experience, educational reformers have argued for growth in measurable performance indicators. Thus, students are objects, and education involves doing things to them (Freire, 1970). Rather than considering the qualitative immediacy of the classroom and nurturing the kinds of relationships needed to promote authentic growth, educators narrow their focus to trajectories that will lead to gains on standardized measures. This two-dimensional image of curriculum objectifies the students and dismisses both the physical an existential conditions within which they live. Further, it objectifies the teachers as instruments administering treatments in largely prescribed ways. As such, teachers and students function as passive bodies—much like the figures found in William Hogarth's engraving, *Gin Lane* (1751), a print designed to warn the working class of London about the evils of gin. In Hogarth's image, villagers share a common space of a London street, yet they are unaware of those around them. With glazed-over, drunken expressions, the villagers in the scene withdraw from each other. A child falls from her mother's breast, unnoticed as she topples into the stairwell. Others on the crowded street are either bloated from their binges or emaciated—neglecting their own bodies as well as those around them. Images of corpses appear throughout the print—one has hung himself and is visible through the cracks in the dilapidated building. Another is being tossed into a cheap coffin. The crowded street strewn with debris and chaos emphasizes the inevitable neglect that pervades spaces where there is no true sense of community (Sennett, 1994).

While Hogarth's scene of disengagement and neglect can be attributed to gin, the comparable disengagement in classrooms today results from a curricular focus on achievement, accountability, and accreditation. When educators define curriculum as trajectories of action and develop curriculum reforms accordingly, they sacrifice the possibility of genuine growth and meaning making for the sake of a false sense of security that comes in the form of aggregate test scores or accreditation benchmarks. They erase the spatial nature of curriculum work in exchange for a simplistic, linear process. As a result, curriculum reform efforts do not offer opportunities for multiple considerations of the complexity of schools and programs. Instead, they force an Etch-a-Sketch mentality upon educators—moving in one specific direction until "experts" turn the knobs and take the stakeholders in another direction. Sadly, as long as educators promote an image of curriculum reform as a trajectory of action, they will always find themselves in a dilemma: Etch-a-Sketch curriculum reform will always fail.

Ironically, schools and universities include images of community within their talk about curriculum reform (DuFour & Eaker, 1998; Shapiro & Levine, 1999). Yet, any real image of community that would be reasonable given the overall nature of curriculum as described above would, at best be interactional, not transactional. As Boyles (2012) notes in his analysis of John Dewey's naturalism and transactional realism, interaction can occur without considering the consequences of the interaction while transactions ensure growth and meaning making. Individuals can interact in passive ways. Teachers can transmit information to students, and students, in true spectator fashion, can receive that information. Even if students later recall the information on an exam, they have, nevertheless, remained passive in the process. As such, much of what passes as teaching and learning—the banking metaphor Paulo Freire (1970) laments—is passive and its participants are, for the most part, disengaged.

In order to shift the nature of education from a series of interactions to authentic transactions, images of curriculum reform must be addressed spatially. As Dewey (1938) argues, "Whatever else organic life is or is not; it is a process of activity that involves an environment. It is a transaction extending beyond the spatial limits of the organism. An organism does not live in an environment; it lives by means of an environment" (p. 25). This is key. How do we create both the conditions and the expectations from which and through which students learn *by means of* an environment, not merely *in* an environment? For this to happen, the environment must be acknowledged as an essential part of the curriculum. Dewey also argued that education is life. It is not preparation for future living, and yet current discourse by policy makers and educators focuses exclusively on future aims. Students are in school to "achieve," and those in P-12 schools are to achieve for the sake of becoming career and college ready while those in colleges and universities are to achieve in order to meet professional proficiencies or to successfully pass a qualifying or certifying exam. Who they are currently and the lives they live are irrelevant.

Curriculum as a Trajectory of Action

How do we shift from images of curriculum as a trajectory of action to images of curriculum as space? What must we give up in order to make this shift? What must we embrace in order to sustain this new image of curriculum? First, we have to be mindful of our complicity regarding how images of curriculum have evolved over the past two to three decades, particularly in relation to P-12 schooling. As curriculum scholars, we accepted the language of standards as largely the exclusive frame of reference for curriculum. We did not consciously and explicitly enlarge the conversation within the context of work that was happening in schools. There was a period in the history of our field when we did offer alternative images of curriculum. Merely peruse old issues of *Educational Leadership* and you will find countless articles where curriculum is framed in terms of experience. Further, curriculum scholars of the seventies and the eighties debated the purpose of schooling. During this period, curriculum deliberations often centered on making experiences meaningful (Tyler, 1978) and maintaining flexibility within the experiences planned (Howard, 1976; Lipsky, 1976). For example, Howard (1976) argued for a state of curriculum wherein

> the teacher-learner relationship is a very personal one, that the teaching and learn-
> ing are human, creative, sometimes emotional acts, that all pupils do not need to
> learn the same things, and that the curriculum must be flexible so that individual
> differences can be accommodated (p. 597).

During this period, curriculum scholars addressed the complexity of schooling and its impact on curriculum (Hunt, 1978). They also discussed the complex relationship between society and schooling (Giroux, 1979). Scholars indicated the need for curriculum to reflect the values and beliefs of society, but curriculum workers should not let those in power within society control the nature and context of curriculum for their own ends. Overall, there was a clear message to educators during this period, curriculum work is complex and is never finished (Fisher & Klein, 1978).

Both the tone and the language of curriculum in *Educational Leadership* began to shift in the eighties. This was due, in large part, to the shifting nature of schooling. There was a significant decline in local control of education as language regarding the technical process of developing curriculum grew and was applied to larger systems of making curriculum decisions: from the classroom and school to the district and then ultimately to the State.

These shifts in the 1980s and early 1990s were merely a foretaste of what was to come. By the early part of this decade, images of curriculum as anything beyond the fodder used to apply "best practices" all but disappeared. Even references to the word "curriculum" in articles in *Educational Leadership* have declined by 74% since the journal's inception. Given the role this journal plays in the knowledge base of most administrators across the country, this tangible decline is a clear indicator that we have lost a foothold in the professional imaginations of the most influential people in schools. They are not thinking about curriculum. The curriculum is the textbook, the standards, and/or the test. The purpose of schooling is not open for debate or even open for enlarging the conversation beyond "achievement."

Thus, the shift from talk of standards and achievement among educational leaders to talk about measuring outcomes and accountability among policy makers and the general public naturally evolved. Attaching those measures to some sign of certainty in terms of teacher quality and school ratings makes sense given human nature. As Dewey (1929/1984) notes, it is human nature to seek out and cling to certainty. Shifting the language about curriculum to constructs that are easily measured and appear to signify something certain plays into our human nature. We can identify a "good" teacher, the "best" schools, and the highest ranked programs simply by referring to a graph or a table. This shift to images of certainty perpetuates our images of school reform as trajectories of action. If curriculum is a given, and if all outcomes of that given curriculum are measureable, then it stands to reason that we can map out a series of steps that would apply to all and will produce the same results. And if it is reasonable to map out a series of steps that would apply to all and produce the same results, then we can hold all equally accountable for achieving common goals.

While curriculum scholars lament this simplistic image of what really happens in schools, we nevertheless must recognize why these images have gained such momentum and appear to be unstoppable in terms of shaping educational policy. Parents and pundits alike have no other options to consider in terms of addressing the education of their children. Much like the uneducated purveyor of a work of art who chooses his or her favorite because it is pretty or because it makes him or her feel good, the general public cannot articulate what they want in education. Winston and Cupchick (1992) note, individuals without background knowledge of art theory have difficulty articulating why they like a particular piece of art. Likewise, parents and policy makers who have no means through which they can see education deeply have no way other than the one provided to articulate what constitutes a good education. In other words, without adequate understanding of the theory and principles that constitute a complex phenomenon, people turn to simplistic responses in the face of that complexity.

Recognizing vs. Perceiving Curriculum

While we cannot mandate coursework in educational theory for every parent and politician, we can create images that help them imagine the function and purpose of schools beyond the current language of measured achievement and world-class standards. In order to do this, we must create within the minds of educators, parents, and the general public a new image of curriculum that pushes the boundaries of the current simplistic calls for achievement. This image must lend itself to tangibility without falling into false notions of certainty. While I am an advocate of seeing curriculum as experience, I do not believe that it is a sustainable image because it is too difficult to attach definitive statements about what should be happening in schools. Further, it runs the risk of playing into the images of "anything goes" that encouraged the accountability movement in the first place. To once again draw upon the wisdom of Dewey (1916), this new image cannot merely be good; it must also be good for something. It must become a frame of reference from which reform and accountability-minded stakeholders can continue to talk about schooling.

By introducing an alternative image for curriculum, we may not significantly influence the degree to which the general public *understands* the complexity of schooling, but we can change the manner in which they *perceive* the nature of schooling. According to Dewey (1994), perception is more than what is immediately encountered. It involves an accumulation of meaning.

It opens up to the potential and provides a "predictive expectancy" (p. 144). Perception is more meaningful than *recognition*. Perception requires pause. It requires an intellectual and, in Panglossian terms, a moral engagement. It jars the complacent figures of Hogarth's scene into some degree of response to those around them. Dewey argues that perception is a vital part of our experience because it helps us to grasp meanings as a whole. We are able to reason according to our range of understanding we have accumulated, and that range is based upon the degree to which we have lingered over complex matters.

Thinking about schooling in terms of achievement and standards really doesn't require thinking at all. It involves recognition of a simplistic measure as a signifier for a false sense of certainty. In other words, it involves *recognition*, not *perception*. Dewey (1934a) laments, "Recognition is perception before it has a chance to develop freely" (p. 52). Further, utility arrests recognition before it can develop into perception. When the basis for our public discourse on education is rooted in recognition of false signifiers of certainty, then the general public is at greater risk for falling prey to meanings crafted by others. How else can we explain the blind adherence to recent policies that hold teachers accountable for so much that is beyond their control?

In contrast, perceiving the nature of education and using a common image to support how we perceive it engages our capacity to imagine something altogether different and better for students. As Dewey (1934b) notes,

> An unseen power controlling our destiny becomes the power of the ideal... The artists, scientist, parent, as far as they are actuated by the spirit of their callings, are controlled by the unseen. For all endeavor for the better is moved by faith in what is possible, not by adherence to the actual (p. 23).

Engaging our public imagination for schooling disrupts habits and vague responses to the world around us. It challenges us to reject false choices perpetuated by simplistic images of accountability. Perceiving curriculum differently can serve as an "edifying discourse" to draw us into the profound, complex, and uncertain (Kierkegaard, 1958). As Jackson (1998) notes, engaging our imaginations in this way "reawakens our sensibilities" (p. 27). We believe engaging our public imagination involves more than merely causing us to see what we have otherwise come to overlook. It also challenges us to see in full that which we have only seen in part, and it draws us into the recognition that certain tensions between school and society cannot be easily reconciled, but that does not mean they should be ignored.

Further, engaging our public imagination to perceive new images of curriculum propels us toward living out our ontological vocation of being in the world more fully because it engages what Garrison (1997) describes as our prophetic capacities:

> Prophets have the capacity to penetrate the veneer of supposedly fixed and final actuality and name what constrains and oppresses us. They expose the aesthetic and moral possibilities that lie beneath the knowledge and unalterable rules and laws. Their poetry is a criticism of life (p. 135).

This capacity, according to Garrison, involves a passionate awareness. It is neither a casual nor a complacent sense of the world around us. It the midst of our encounter with this image of curriculum, we turn outward and respond—we act upon the world we perceive (Greene, 1995). To this end, our work becomes transactional, not merely interactional (Boyles, 2012). As Freire (1970) argues, we "insert" ourselves within our world and see ourselves belonging to it. We position ourselves as subjects who can act upon the world in the midst of its ambiguity and uncertainty. We are able to do this because of our imaginative vision (Garrison, 1997). Our response to schools, and to the world, becomes a rhythmic enterprise—grounding and swelling between harmony and disharmony as a "more and aesthetic as well as intellectual journey" (Garrison, 1997, p. 135).

The numb villagers of Hogarth's *Gin Lane* did not explicitly set out to disengage with their community. The disengagement was a result of the gin. The gin was the controlling variable and the havoc it wreaked upon the village happened to be the subsequent outcome. Similarly, well-meaning stakeholders involved in education do not set out to dehumanize teachers and blame the impoverished students for the conditions in which they live. Stakeholders who seek reform in schools are limited by the means through which reform is recognized and measured. As noted previously, recognizing reform through false notions of certainty can lead to interaction between stakeholders and the work of schools, but it will not lead to transactions, and interactions do not lead stakeholders to consider consequences or complexity (Boyles, 2012).

The Role of Metaphor in Engaging our Professional Imaginations

Metaphors serve as effective tools through which we can explore the complex nature of phenomena. They can help us move from recognition to perception.

In other words, an effective metaphor can help us engage our professional imaginations when addressing issues of education. The symbolic meanings we create function as metaphors within our daily contexts, and, as Scheffler (1997) notes, "… the metaphorical description itself serves as an invitation to its originator and to others, to develop its ramifications" (p. 70). The met-aphorical function of understanding our experiences should not be underesti-mated. According to Langer (1960), metaphors are the most striking evidence of "abstractive seeing." She notes, "… if ritual's the cradle of language, met-aphor is the law of its life. It is the force that makes is essentially relational" (p. 141). Similarly, the power of metaphors themselves should not be over-looked. As Lakoff and Johnson (1980) note, what we know about the world around us is shaped by our social reality and the manner in which it shapes our experiences. Since so much of our social reality is understood in metaphorical terms, metaphors themselves determine what is real for us.

Metaphors provide powerful spaces in which we can explore the aesthetic dimension of our epistemological enterprise, for they offer a public medium through which we collectively come to know our shared lived experiences. As such, they take us beyond conventional understandings to create new images and new possibilities. Metaphors engage our professional imaginations in four ways. First, they are not nor can they be utilitarian in the sense of a specified trajectory in response to an event. There is no certain way to respond to phenomena as it is represented metaphorically. Second, metaphors prevent us from categorizing the subject of our inquiry—whether as ideas, symbols, or people. Further, metaphors force us to hold onto multiple meanings of our symbols and experiences and thus of ourselves. As a result, the simultaneous exploration of diversity and community evident within a democracy come to life in our metaphorical understandings and our shared experiences. Finally, metaphorical knowing offers a space in which we can dwell. As we take in the metaphorical understandings of our shared experiences, we recognize that our conceptual system of understanding is only partially embodied in the experiences we share—otherwise the metaphor ceases to become the vehicle of reality and becomes, instead, reality itself (Lakoff & Johnson, 1980).

Metaphor serves a vital function in the manner in which we encounter ambiguous identities. As Ricoeur (1975) notes, metaphor does not initiate comparisons or categorizations of multiple meanings. Instead, metaphor pro-vokes abstraction—inquiry into possible significance felt by the existence of multiple meanings. By virtue of our lived experience, multiple meanings and identities interact, and metaphor is able to hold the fullness and complexity of this interaction. Thus who we are, both individually and collectively, is not relegated to simplistic categories or judgments, but instead is poised for possibility. According to Ricoeur (1975), "To present man 'as acting' and all things 'as an act'—such could well be the *ontological* function of metaphorical discourse, in which every dormant potentiality of existence appears *as* blossoming forth, every latent capacity for action *as* actualized" (p. 143, italics in original).

Curriculum as Spaces

Seeing curriculum as spaces offers images that help us respond to schooling and to one another as we ponder purpose, potential, and significance within our work. It elevates the unanticipated and the immeasurable to our consciousness and makes it a deliberate part of our discourse. Further, perceiving curriculum as space reminds us that our work is always mediated by historical, cultural, and political contexts, and it unfolds according to students' lived experiences. Shifting images of curriculum to space also reminds us that we do not necessarily and directly enact change within our students. We cannot see the world in shallow, controllable, and measurable terms. Instead, we alter physical, psychological, and moral conditions that are shared with others, and in the process we too are changed. We affect our shared space with a faith that the conditions we create and support will bring about the dreams we have for one another. We engender possibilities by virtue of the spaces we create, and we realize the potential of those possibilities to the degree that we consciously strive to articulate our shared dreams, hopes, and fears.

Framing curriculum in terms of space also provides opportunities for alternative measures of success. It takes away the power of test scores in and of themselves. Consider the manner in which the work of architects is judged. Architecture is judged both by its quality as well as its beauty. As Blake (1996) notes, the first life of a structure is judged according to its function. Does it work? Were the designs accurate? Does the structure function as it was designed? Without this level of quality, the structure is not viable. However, the life of a building does not stop with quality. It lives on through its beauty. Thus, its second life is judged as a work of art. What is the relationship between the structure and its environment? How does the structure influence the design of future buildings? How do elements of the structure continue, generation after generation, to take the occupant by surprise in their coherence with nature or with the relationship between beauty and function?

Framing curriculum in terms of space shifts our images of schooling from trajectories of action. Trajectories of action limit our discussion about school experiences to "how to" do something or the "best practices." They exclude experiences students should have and ignore the conditions we need to support in order to ensure that students have highly educative experiences. Considering the nature of schooling exclusively as trajectories of action perpetuates linear and narrow views of what teachers and students do. As such, our work resembles an Etch-a-Sketch: moving in a particular direction (as dictated by a model or mandate) until we are compelled to change to another direction. This mindset compels us to move, to change, and to implement.

Most importantly, framing curriculum in terms of space opens up the possibility of engaging in meaningful dialogue about purpose. Curriculum as space draws us in to explore what we value for ourselves and for others, and it creates the opportunity to achieve a clear manifestation of that purpose together. As Cosgrove notes when reviewing the life work of Mies van der Rohe,

> Architecture, when done right, embodies a civilization's values and aspirations; it shows what *mattered* to a given group of people in a given time in history, and translates an artist's vision into tangible, lasting form (http://life.time.com/culture/architect-mies-van-der-rohe-and-the-poetry-of-purpose/#8).

However, the purpose of education can be, and has been, narrowly conceived and grossly misguided over the past several decades, and sadly, this is clearly evident in the spaces our students and teachers are forced to occupy. Policy makers and business leaders have created the spaces in which schooling is taking place, and yet we blame the structure itself—the space created by those in power—instead of challenging those who designed it. We need to recognize the role of the spaces we create so that we can accept responsibility for those spaces rather than blaming the physical structures once they are erected as if they—in their inanimate state—are to blame for the problems.

Dewey (1934a) argues that buildings that lack character, or as he characterized it, packing box architecture, was a result of a lack of character within the architects who designed it. He argued that you cannot fix the structures without first addressing the character of the architects. Mehaffy and Salingaros (2013) concur. They note, "The ugliness and disorder of our present human environment is certainly related to the ugliness and disorder due to the damage we have created in the natural environment" (p. 3). They critique geometrical fundamentalism of modern architecture, and they point to the corporate and political influence over architectural design and urban planning where Le Corbusier and others focused on geometric simplicity and perpetuation of urban sprawl in order to shift the social norms toward a "desire-culture." For example, they share an excerpt from Le Corbusier's (1967) image of an ideal urban space:

> The cities will be part of the country; I shall live 30 miles from my office in one direction, under a pine tree; my secretary will live 30 miles away from it too, in the other direction, under another pine tree. We shall both have our own car. We shall use up tires, wear out road surfaces and gears, consume oil and gasoline. All of which will necessitate a great deal of work..... enough for all (p. 74).

Mehaffey and Salingaros (2013) lament that the line of reasoning that accompanied much of the modernist movement and the urban design influenced by it undermined human connections and erased a sense of community. They note, "Moderism's fundamentalist geometry destroyed architecture's capacity to form significantly cohesive wholes. Instead, we were left with a disordered collection of abstract art pieces—forced, in effect, to live in someone else's increasing disorganized sculpture gallery" (p. 4). They further argue that humans became part of the segregated pieces. In this new desire-based culture, we were able to move away from the city and away from others who were not like us and feed our consumerist tendencies with the big-box stores we found within those suburbs.

Yet, the structures themselves are not to blame for the fact that these re-imagined spaces profoundly impact how we live and work, or more to the point, how we now live to work. We cannot blame the sprawling packing-box architecture for undermining a sense of community and perpetuating a consumerist culture any more than we can shake our heads at homes built without front porches and subdivisions without sidewalks and consider them reason why we no longer connect with our neighbors (Kunstler, 1994). These new spaces are what they are by design. The architects and city planners designed them with clear purposes in mind: most of which were centered on economic forces. When we acknowledge that spaces exist by design and that designers create them, then we can question more thoughtfully the nature of those designs. When we achieve a level of evaluating the spaces of schooling, then we can engage our imaginations regarding what these spaces *should* be.

Schooling as Heterotopia

We need more traction to engage our professional imaginations within curriculum spaces. We need to recognize that our ontological vocation involves approximating ideals for ourselves and for our students. We cannot put forth a narrative about schooling that deals exclusively with utopian ideals. Otherwise we have no way of engaging those who are in corporate boardrooms, state departments, and classrooms and who must focus on the daily realities of schooling. We must find an alternative image that allows us to wrestle with current realities without sacrificing educational ideals. To this end, we can imagine educational spaces as heterotopias.

Foucault distinguishes between utopias and heterotopias. In his 1967 lecture to architects, he notes that utopias are not real. They provide images of perfection, and while we may wish to discuss curriculum in terms of utopian ideals, in the end, they are imaginary. In contrast, Foucault points to real spaces—enacted utopias. These heterotopias embrace the ideal and the real simultaneously. While they are outside of reality, they can signify the real world. Foucault characterized the relationship between utopia and heterotopia in terms of a mirror. We may stand before a mirror and see what we could be in its reflection—an image of possibility. This allows us to re-examine who we are in the world and approximate the utopian image we see. To this end, the mirror represents utopia while our engagement with the mirror and the manner in which we change to reflect what we see in the mirror represents heterotopia. He notes, "it makes this place that I occupy at the moment when I look at myself in the glass at once absolutely real, connected with all the space that surrounds it, and absolutely unreal, since in order to be perceived it has to pass through this virtual point which is over there" (Foucault, 1967, p. 4).

Heterotopias can sustain multiple functions, even if some of the functions are incompatible. To this end, we do not deny the need for curriculum to help prepare students for the future, but we do not stop there. We argue that that is merely one purpose of education, and as such it may create tension with other purposes such as building a democratic community (Dewey, 1915/1944) or helping students to become more authentic beings (Greene, 1971). By creating the opportunity to hold these conflicting images simultaneously, schools as heterotopias urge us to engage with one another in relation to these tensions.

Further, heterotopias can embrace the historical nature of our identities without relegating us to be finished fixtures within a historical point and time.

As Huebner (1967) notes, the notion of time arises out of our existence. Human life is made up of how the past and the future are brought into the moment. Our temporal nature, as Huebner argues, is never fixed. Heterotopias embrace both the "perpetual and indefinite accumulation of time in an immobile place" (Foucault, 1967/1984, p. 7) as well as the temporal and emerging nature of our lives.

Thus, schooling as heterotopia allows us to encounter difference in ways that does not erase it. This state is consistent with the democratic ideal and it is a necessary condition for our aesthetic receptivity to the world (Schoolman, 2001). According to Schoolman (2001), our aesthetic receptivity is contingent upon the context in which we are situated. If that context is not democratic, we are unable to accept differences and act in concert within and among those differences. He notes, "Without democracy… individuality is unable to become aesthetic" (p. 22). Democratic spaces allow us to encounter one another more fully because it offers both mimetic and moral dimensions to our collective lives. Schoolman notes that democracy entails a mimetic dimension whereby we take in and maintain difference. Whatever may constitute our individuality does not become subsumed within a larger collective identity. We do not melt into some homogenous identity nor do groups of individuals fall neatly and absolutely into clearly established categories. He notes, "For each individual, differences are pluralized or multiplied; hence for the mass, differences are undiminished" (p. 277). As a result, we are aware of our collective identity while we simultaneously seek out the complex identities of others. Seeking differences becomes an aesthetic impulse in our lives and work with one another.

Transaction, Disfiguring, and the Moral Dimension of Curriculum

While metaphors facilitate the mimetic dimension of our understanding, consciousness of differences within the context of shared experiences, in and of itself, is insufficient. With metaphor alone, we can remain intellectually engaged yet morally complacent. In other words, our work as educators can still neglect authentic transactions. Bowers (1980) offers the following critique of metaphors to warn us of our potential to stay disengaged:

In the face of a reified symbolic world—of which "freedom," "data," and "inequality" are examples—the individual loses sight of his intentionality in how such metaphors are to be interpreted and acted on in the context of everyday life. The alienation of man from the symbolic world that is constructed and externalized is in Nietzsche's sense the ultimate expression of will to power, but expressed in a manner that does not involve taking existential responsibility (p. 274).

To move beyond a mere intellectual exercise, we need to actively seek out tensions and significance in our shared lives and respond to them collectively. This seeking out and responding can be viewed in terms of Taylor's (1992) notion of disfiguration—a collective act that conjoins abstraction and figuration. It involves seeking the eternal and immutable within our collective lives while simultaneously holding onto the contingent. Taylor (1992) also notes,

> Disfiguring enacts denigration in the real figure, image, form, and representation ... revelation and concealment as well as presence and absence are interwoven in such a way that every representation is both a re-presentation and a depresentation (p. 7).

While we see our identities within the metaphorical spaces of the curriculum, we deliberately isolate the essence of individual meanings in order to perceive ourselves and publicly wrestle with who we are in relation to one another. We do not attempt to find answers. Instead, we endeavor to identify and hold on to tensions that result from irreconcilable meanings while simultaneously identifying patterns of reason stemming from the ambiguous nature of what we see. We use our individual and collective identities with and against themselves in order to respond to the referential enactment of those identities upon our shared experiences. This requires two very different tasks that combine the aesthetic and the epistemological in a collective moral act. We wrestle with what our identities mean to us personally and collectively while we simultaneously critique what these identities do to us when they are used by others.

This shift toward transactional being with one another calls for a radical ontology. According to Carlson (1982), we need to return to a hermeneutic rationality that summons us to seek out and face anxiety, and this ontologically grounded anxiety should be a vital part of the curriculum. He contends, "The task of critical educators is to help individuals face ontologically-grounded anxiety, for it is only in the face of anxiety that one is empowered to act more authentically and recapture that which has been appropriated" (Carlson, 1982, p. 209).

I would add to Carlson's definition, however, the moral necessity of seeing ourselves as both the subject and the object of that anxiety. It is not just a matter of pointing to what others have done to us—how those in power have appropriated the curriculum and are using it for their own purposes. It is just a much an examination of how our collective lives have played a part in the creation and maintenance of our identities and how we should respond accordingly. Thus, in order to engage in curricular transactions, we must be willing to remain ill at ease. We do not engage one another in efforts to solve problems. Instead, we recognize and take responsibility for the problems while realizing that they cannot be solved. To do this, we must maintain a sense of ideological vulnerability and compassion as a community in order to fully address the implications of who we are and the significance of the multiple (and often conflicting) meanings we share (Adair Breault, 2003).

Conclusion: Curriculum as Radical Transactions

In Audrey Lorde's poem, "To My Daughter the Junkie on the Train," Lorde describes a woman's experience returning home from a PTA meeting on a subway. A young woman "with a horse in her brain." slumps down beside this woman and uses her as a pillow as she drifts off to sleep. When it is time for the woman to exit the train, she extends a glance of compassion toward the wretched figure. Her offer to help is met with "terrible technicolor laughter," and all the mothers up and down the aisle of the subway car turn away— unable to gaze upon their own failures as mothers displayed in this image of a junkie. The compassionate gaze offered by the woman was a transaction- al, aesthetic, and moral act. It reached beyond the mere utility of assistance to make a connection with something that was part of the woman but had been lost.

It is one thing to be in a constant state of awareness of the complexity of curriculum and the ways in which our collective identities contribute to that complexity; it is another to do something about it. In other words, we can engage our professional imaginations without taking moral responsibility for our work. How do we open ourselves to the ambiguity and tensions found within curriculum in a meaningful way? How do we avoid the false promis- es of certainty? First, we must recognize that the mimetic dimension of our identities is a very real part of our work together, but it alone is not suffi- cient. We cannot merely recognize the complexity and tensions found within our shared lived experiences and yet, like the women on Lorde's train, turn away and reject our role in the tensions. Instead, we must bind our moral vocation with our mimetic. We must seek out the brutality that is common to us all—recognizing that which is irreconcilable within our identities and then hold on to that which is irreconcilable. Not only must we extend that compassionate gaze in a single instance, as did the woman on the train. We must also be in a constant state of anticipation to extend such a gaze. It is that expectation of encounter with the ambiguous that makes the aesthetics of knowing and being a moral enterprise that enhances not only the personal but also the public spaces.

· 2 ·

THE AESTHETIC MOMENT
IN EDUCATION

The expression of personal and communal practices and perspectives, through art, has never been far from either human, or even their ancestors' experiences. While the earliest known art produced by humans, a necklace of shell beads found in Israel, dates to about 100,000 years ago, the discovery of the Berekhat Ram figurine, also found in Israel, seems to date from between 200,000–470,000 years ago, perhaps predating the time of the Neanderthals. Yet, even this art seems young when compared to the Acheulean hand axes that were created 1.8 million years ago. Whether hand axes rise to the level of art might be debatable. What is certain, however, is that archaeologists have found elements of symmetry and composition that add nothing to the effectiveness of the hand axe except a sense of beauty (Kohn & Mithen, 1999; Nowell & Chang, 2009). Art, then, has been around for a long time!

Prehistoric art, however, did not just happen. While there are many interpretations of meaning, archaeologists have speculated that the tiny figurines, often depicting women with exaggerated reproductive features and collectively called Venuses, are easily portable icons of security or fertility (White, 2008). Cave paintings, for their part, are perhaps more consistent with rituals associated with a form of Shamanism that arose during the Upper Paleolithic age (Clottes & Lewis-Williams, 1998). Indeed, the ways in which animals were painted on cave walls, the universality of images, and the mixing of a complex cosmos in which two worlds—the physical and the mystical—exit side by side are indicative of early human efforts to both understand and control their worlds through spirituality and other forms of meaning making. Perhaps more importantly, Gregory Curtis (2008) suggests that regardless of meaning, the creation and re-creation of early art depended upon a passing down of skills from one generation to the next. In short, the joining of craft, material, and meaning formed the world's first art curriculum. Art was present, meaningful, and part of cultural traditions!

While theories that seek to ascertain the meaning of early art abound, in reality the passage of time precludes finding a definitive answer. It is equally impossible to reconstruct conversations that early humans and/or their ancestors might have had relative to the art produced within their communities. It is not, however, impossible to imagine that these conversations took place. As nomadic peoples wandered the landscape and happened upon the caves and encampments where art was made, was present, or had been left behind, whether due to hasty retreats or purposeful testimonies to spirituality, there was in all likelihood conversations about the aesthetic qualities of art, or in more simple terms, beauty and meaning. Whether concerning shell beads, figurines, cave paintings, poetry, or even hand axes, humans have, in all probability, long discussed, debated, decried, and praised favorite "artists" and wondered aloud at the meaning of it all.

Yet to consider appreciation of art, in its various forms, as simply a question of beauty misses the potential of art as well as other experiences to shape and guide lives. As early humans and their ancestors encountered new forces of nature, often mysterious and threatening, there is no doubt that they sought ways to influence and control the world they inhabited. The making and viewing of art, then, was probably more than a simple act of appreciation of beauty and craft. Making and viewing art was possibly accompanied by important and perhaps troubling realizations of one's place in the world. Whether to appease or control the spirit world, to ensure fertility, or to praise ample harvest, art and other experiences provoked an aesthetic moment of mutuality from which a transcendent sense of self is invented. This notion of the aesthetic moment is, of course, not far removed from Bakhtin's (1981) as well as Cissna and Anderson's (1998) concept of the dialogical moment in which commonalities are new ways of seeing are forged within long conversations.

In considering the importance of dialog in forging new ways of being, it is not difficult to construe discussions, both historical and contemporary, about aesthetics, about the connections between lived experiences and art, as one long conversation centering on meaning making within and between individuals. The purpose of this chapter is to unpack the meaning of aesthetics and to uncover the promise of the aesthetic moment, particularly as it pertains to place-based education. In short, we seek to understand the aesthetic moment's potential to disrupt numbing influences of rampant consumerism, information overload, sounds of sirens in the streets, and DIS-placed curricula that do not attend or add meaning to the lives of an increasing number of American youth. The effort entails the beginning of a long and complex conversation that, as Pinar (2012) suggests, includes and encourages discussions about curriculum that occur across time and on many different levels. Further, these conversations are based on dialogical processes that privilege multiple voices and perspectives. Given the importance of locality, these conversations are couched within sense of community, a localized and place-based exploration of self, society, and context that stands in opposition to a DIS-placed education that ignores the importance of both space and place in communities.

Even as we note the pivotal role that conversations plays in self-discovery, we also realize that the frailty of language to convey meaning, to express thoughts, and to effect change has been problematized by Jacques Derrida, Michel Foucault, and within education, Joseph Schwab. Indeed, language at once frames who we are, ensnaring individuals in self-perpetuating identities while also providing the means to explore alternatives, shatter barriers that inhibit physical and intellectual border crossing, and raise consciousness beyond taken-for-granted attitudes. Language, in short, captures current experiences, sorts individuals into in- and out-groups, and offers hope for new idioms that provoke change.

Following the lead of Jacques Rancière, we challenge the territorialization and control of language, history, and promise that forbids educational and social heresy. In short, we seek a sort of "dissensus" that questions and disrupts the well-organized spaces and "senso comune" of the hegemonic state and which also gives rise to a new linguistic idiom replete with the potential to explore the personal while concurrently inviting a discourse of the common. Indeed, while we recognize the importance of the personal, autobiographical language that Pinar champions, we wish to speak more directly of language as a social event which privileges the notion of language as a dialogical process that occurs within a range of cultural, institutional, educational, and political diversity that is simultaneously bewildering and promising, but which is ultimately couched within a Deweyan notion of community that fosters individual awareness within a nurturing and meaningful community.

In considering the aesthetic question, we wish to both recognize and disrupt the important and long historical linkages between education and art in its many forms. For the former, recognition of connections between art and education, we are cognizant that artists, art critics, and art theorists have long explored aesthetics from multiple vantage points including highly atomized notions of perfect form and composition as well as holistic approaches that promote overall perception of beauty. For the latter, disrupting connections between art and education, we question pedagogical emphasis that aesthetic education places on a surprisingly rule-bound conceptualization of the "art-lived experience-transformative moment" syntax that often frames aesthetic pedagogy. Indeed, within the rather conventional approach to aesthetic education, transformative practice is cordoned off into a small and ever diminishing slice of the curricular pie that is quickly and easily deformed by the pressure of and reliance on an orthodox modernism that transmits, restores, and reinforces traditional hierarchies through the act of schooling. Indeed, we believe that whether in the world of art or education, instruments of socio-political reproduction are present and well-entrenched.

To continue, however, let us return to the beginning, to the voices that inform, shape, and guide our conversations. The history of the study of the relationship between art, pedagogy, and life has been explored in numerous anthologies (Adams, 1971; Dickie, Sclafani, & Roblin, 1989; Rader, 1979; Ross, 1984) and has long been a part of the human experience. We might, within this long tradition, identify four distinct periods that serve as a general guide to our conversation. First, the ancient Greeks, as is so often the case in Western philosophy, began the modern conversation with Plato's dialogues which were followed by Aristotle's *Poetics* and eventually Plotinus' Neo-Platonic revival. For the Greeks, and particularly Plato and Aristotle, aesthetics had an important pedagogical component. Whether serving as the principles on which the choice of appropriate "teaching material" for the ruling class, as for Plato, or as guidelines for the production of good poetry, as for Aristotle, both of these brilliant Greek philosophers described rather prescriptive pedagogical functions for aesthetics. Nonetheless, these voices are the origins of all subsequent discussions about aesthetic philosophy and form the basis for the exploration of the aesthetic conversation.

While the ancient Greeks dominated philosophical traditions for almost 2000 years, a second phase began in the late 17th century with the Age of the

Enlightenment and its focus on reason and individual as opposed to tradition. This movement, as described by Immanuel Kant in his famous essay *What Is Enlightenment?* (Kant, 1784), was simply the freedom for humans to use their native intelligence. Basing their epistemologies on the application of reason and rationality to every human problem, philosophers as well-known and influential as Kant, Alexander Baumgarten, Gotthold Lessing, and Wilhelm Hegel (among many others), explored aesthetics as the marriage of reason to the senses. While later philosophers, especially of the Romantic Movement, would criticize the Enlightenment for the impossibility of an overly ambitious rational agenda, the works of these men remain foundational in the field of aesthetics. While the Enlightenment added infinitely important avenues for exploring aesthetics to the conversation, it did turn the conversation toward metaphysical approaches to epistemology and ever so slightly away from the prescriptive pedagogical approaches to art, broadly defined, found in antiquity.

The third set of voices, added under the significant influence of John Dewey, reasserted a pedagogical position for aesthetics as well as a repositioning of the field toward pragmatic and naturalistic philosophies that privilege a connection between lived conditions, knowledge of self, and life within communities. Indeed, in *Art as Experience*, Dewey (1934a) applied his mature naturalistic view of intellectual and social environments as well as his distrust of dualisms in the pursuit of a clear and intimate connection between art, life, and community. Dewey sought, in the pages of *Art as Experience*, to directly connect art to the lived experiences of humans. He rejected, in short, art as the property of the intellectual elite and promoted a view that associated pleasurably viewing of art with the immediate and lived conditions of the viewer. For contemporary notions of aesthetics, including those of Maxine Greene, Dewey's influence, especially within subfield of educational aesthetics, remains both present and strong.

The final voices, represented by works and thoughts of Jacques Rancière, return to many of the themes of the Enlightenment, including the connections between the double meanings of sense (sensory perceptions and cognitive processes). For Rancière, the admittedly double entendre "partage du sensible" allows for proactive pedagogies that seek equality among all members of a community. Indeed, the plurality of pedagogies and aesthetics, whether political, social, or education, reinvigorate aesthetics as transformative practices across a myriad of social ills. These pluralities offer aesthetics as an eclectic set of practices that build on past traditions while also reclaiming aesthetics from its emphasis on art and beauty. In returning, in a sense, to aesthetics as lived sensorial perceptions, as in its Greek origins, contemporary educational aesthetics privileges curricula that are RE-placed within communities of sense (Hinderliter, Kaizen, Maimon, Mansoor, & McCormick, 2009) and which offer an antidote to the increasingly sterile and anesthetic curricula found in contemporary schooling.

Back, to the beginning. The ancient Greeks were among the first to formally explore the relationships between art and life and to assign some pedagogical implications to the connections. While is it often difficult to establish where Socrates' thoughts end and those of Plato and other students begin, he is considered the originator of modern conceptualizations of aesthetics. From the accounts of the Athenian general Xenophon, in his *Memorabilia*, Socrates adamantly believed that absolute beauty was but a myth. In a highly rationalistic as well as subject-oriented approach to beauty, Socrates is presented as suggesting that beauty is inherently connected to usefulness. To illustrate, Socrates noted that "even a dung basket...should be called beautiful if it is well adapted to be useful in its way" (Richter, 1967, 2). This admittedly crude example demonstrates, rather succinctly, Socrates' overriding principle of that which is well adapted to a task is by consequence beautiful.

Plato, too, gives voice to Socrates' (or perhaps his own) view of aesthetics. While early Socratic dialogues, such as *Hippias Major*, explore the question of beauty, eventually settling on a less than satisfactory definition of "that which is both profitable and pleasurable," more mature views emerge in the *Symposium*, *The Republic*, and *Phaedo*. In these, Plato suggests that Socrates developed a more full understanding of aesthetics, including the role that art plays in nurturing the ruling class and promoting a just and civil society. With an underlying belief that art could be enjoyed and appreciated through contemplation of form (including sound and color), Plato nonetheless has Socrates point out that life is not about simple pleasure. Rather, life has a higher purpose—"enlightenment through rational inquiry and, ultimately, through direct encounter with Absolute Truth" (Richter, 1967, 28).

While Plato had condemned both imitative arts and vulgar poetry to the scrapheap of history (c.f., the *Phaedrus*), Aristotle sought to resurrect the arts and particularly poetry. Even in accepting many of Plato's premises, he discards the Platonic disdain for imitative art by taking for granted their reality. Aristotle views, quite contrary to Plato, art objects not as copies of things, but as things real by their own accord. Further, he suggests that art, like politics, is a purposeful act that is reflective of the highest fulfillment of man's intelligence—the capacity to create. Moving ever so slightly from art to beauty, Aristotle, in *The Poetics*, promotes a rather rational and normative conceptualization of beauty being characterized by formal properties, including order, symmetry, and other mathematical measurements (Richter, 1967).

An essential question for the early Greeks was the contentious relationship between inspiration and rhetorical mastery. As a brief aside, we note that in ancient Greece, the conflict between the sophists, or those who believed that an appeal to the emotions was a vital part of argument and rhetoricians who believed in the ultimate power and goodness of arguing and reasoning from reason and logical stances. Longinus connects the art of rhetoric with inspiration through sublimity, noting specifically that a sublime moment flashes as though it were a bolt of lightning that scatters thought and provides a moment of possibility as ideas and meaning are re-organized (Adams, 1971). While Kant, and others, offered their own perceptions of sublimity, Longinus's pre-occupation with the audience remained a constant in later and more developed works.

The second chorus, added to the conversation, came as part of the Age of the Enlightenment and served, in the mind of Friedrich von Schiller, as the true cradle for the exploration of aesthetic theories. While there is considerable debate over whether modern aesthetics began in England with the Earl of Shaftesbury's rhapsodizing on ideal beauty or in Germany with Alexander Baumgarten's efforts to reconcile his love of poetry with rational thought, there is no doubt that the 18th and 19th centuries brought new ways of seeing to life. Principal among these, again as Schiller noted, was recognition that beauty is one of the primary means to create unity between the abstract concept of mind and the reality of the world of senses. Such noted and notable philosophers as Gotthold Lessing, Alexander Baumgarten, Immanuel Kant, and Wilhelm Hegel added significant voices to the expanding conversation on aesthetics. Working primarily within the epistemological structure of the Age of Enlightenment, that is a desire for rationality and order, these men hewed new conceptualization of aesthetics that were often derived from Plato and which continue to serve as the basis of contemporary discussions. Indeed, while expressing the concept in a myriad of ways, these thinkers, in exploring the potency of the union of mind and senses, collectively settled upon a pedagogical practice that moved from an affirmation to a negation and then to a re-affirmation with new insights. It is indeed an interesting testimony to the quality of the concepts proposed by Kant and the others that this pedagogical system remains prevalent in the contemporary philosophies of Jacques Rancière and others.

While much was added to the conversation between the time of Aristotle and the 18th century, the need for brevity forces us to ignore many important philosophers, including Saint Thomas Aquinas, Alexander Pope, Edmund Burke, and many others. With this in mind, we can begin adding the voices of the second chorus with the rising tide of the Enlightenment and a re-centering of philosophy on reason; intellectuals begin rethinking an overreliance on tradition as the bedrock of thought and action. Riding this new wave of intellectualism and following the rational tradition of Descartes, Leibniz, and Wolff, Alexander Gottlieb Baumgarten considered his dueling and seemingly incompatible interests—reason and art—in *Reflections on Poetry* (1735), his now famous doctoral dissertation. Baumgarten suggested that the difference between philosophy and the other arts was a matter of cognitive complexity. While philosophical inquiry focused on conceptual distinctions between ideas and availed itself of higher cognitive faculties, the purpose of inquiry into the nature of art emanated from a need to explain and explore perceptual vividness that is perceived by the lower cognitive faculty of sensuous perception. To reconcile these seemingly incompatible pursuits, a new science—aesthetics—was required. Within *Reflections* as well as his more mature and considered *Aesthetica* (1750), Baumgarten presented his conclusions that aesthetics is not only concerned with notions of beauty, but also the art of thinking and discovering how beautiful objects are created. In connecting the subjectiveness of sensuous knowledge (or beauty) with the rational search for a logic of creation, Baumgarten collapsed art and philosophy, at least within the aesthetic imagination, into a single and understandable concept.

Although slightly older than Baumgarten, Gotthold Ephraim Lessing (1729–1781) seems the next step in our concise genealogy of aesthetics. Although Lessing had expected to become, like his father, a pastor in the Lutheran church, his passion for theatre soon carved out a new path. With critical successes, such as *Miss Sara Sampson* and a critical essay, *Letters Concerning Recent German Literature*, under his belt, Lessing turned his attention to the limits of arts of poetry and painting. In *Laocoön*, Lessing defines and defends art as autonomous and separate from daily acts. Yet, he also acknowledges their importance in man's attempt to "represent and to interpret life and nature" (Richter, 1967, p. 109). It is, in fact, art's ability to connect man to a pregnant moment, or the precise moment that man's imagination is freed to explore self-awareness with a heightened level of intensity (Donahue, 2005) that underscores the importance of art to man. Lessing's task, no small endeavor, seems to be aimed at constructing an aesthetic theory that seeks a rational understanding of the qualities that make great art both pure and beautiful while also meaningful, inspiring, and perhaps transcendental.

No genealogy, no matter how short, would be complete without a discussion of Immanuel Kant (1724–1804) and *The Critique of Judgment*. In his third critique, Kant proposes an aesthetic theory, expanded upon from *The Critique of Pure Reason*, which opposes teleological and aesthetic judgments—that is, those judgments that consider the ultimate purpose of an object (teleological) and those that consider an object's esoteric nature (aesthetic). Within this framework, we sense two important nuances. First, all canonical judgments of value and beauty, which might be considered external objective criteria, are rejected in favor of an appreciation of and emotive response to the object. This, in turn, places focus on the internality of an object and begins to dismiss the subjectivity of the perceiver. Yet even so, Kant could not fully divorce subjectively and personal autonomy from the calculus that frames beauty. Indeed, his theory of aesthetic judgment, taken from Book One of *The Critique of Judgment*, suggests that rational judgment can be aesthetic if the perceiver is aware that judgments of beauty are being filtered through personal feelings, thereby rendering them rational. As Alex Means (2010) suggests, Kant dedicated a significant portion of his third critique "puzzling through" the inherent contradictions between the autonomy of the perceiver and the internality of the object. Means (2010) concluded, in short that "while Kant allowed the temporary disarticulation of one's evaluative frames within the aesthetic encounter, he would have this moment of disinterested interest rapidly reinscribed within a legislative structure of rational judgment" (p. 1089).

It is no small understatement that Kant's œuvre provoked a flurry of positive and negative responses both prior to his death and to this day. Responses to Kant, couched within a more rational approach to philosophy, define the next round of voices added to the aesthetic question. Indeed, Friedrich Wilhelm von Schelling (1775–1854) and Georg Wilhelm Hegel (1770–1831), perhaps the best-known Kantian critics, seemed to favor an approach that was less metaphysical and more approach based on connections between reason and reality. Schilling, for his part, rejected the division of the subject and object, focusing instead on the aesthetic practice of joining the perceiver and the perceived (Adams, 1971). Hegel, while deeply indebted to Kant for much of his own philosophical thoughts (Smith, 1973), nonetheless criticized him for what he called an overly formalistic epistemological approach as well as a focus on the abstract and unsubstantiated that rendered Kant's conclusions

meaningless. Hegel, in fact, favored a rational approach to philosophical inquiry that created direct connections between human reason and experiences.

Following in the footsteps of Hegel, John Dewey explored questions of
the nature of knowledge and the role of philosophy in the human experience
and more specifically, for our purposes, meaning of aesthetics in life. As is well
known, John Dewey (1859–1952) formed, along with Charles Sanders Peirce
(1839–1914) and William James (1842–1910), the early American pragmatic
movement. In this philosophical tradition, the core maxim, first articulated
by Peirce (Peirce, 1992), noted the importance of clarifying the contents of
any hypothesis by following it to a logical conclusion. Only by discovering
the consequences of an idea could we truly and fully understand the concept.
More fundamentally, perhaps, pragmatism provided an important epistemological frame for dissolving the seeming contradictions between what James
(1907) called the "tough minded" who have an unwavering commitment
to empirical science and the "tender minded" whose work has an a priori
commitment to the human mind. Given Dewey's concern that traditional
epistemologies divorced thought from the world to which it was supposedly
linked, it is not surprising that he embraced pragmatism as the avenue toward
the re-harmonization of divergent and seemingly contradictory inputs.

James, Peirce, and Dewey all argued, through the pragmatic lens and
in their own unique ways that earlier philosophical traditions had erred in
believing in the distinctiveness of experiences and cognition. In many of his
early works, namely Is Logic a Dualistic Science? (Dewey, 1890) and The Present
Position of Logical Theory (Dewey, 1891), Dewey explored theories of knowledge along the parameters set by Hegel with a specific interest in disabusing
his audience of the notion that data stand apart from thought. Yet, as Dewey
matured, he embraced a naturalistic, as opposed to strictly logical, approach
to philosophy that was based on Darwinism and its close alignment between
organisms and the environments they inhabit. Contrary to some traditional avenues of explanation, Dewey came to see an ecological relationship
between thought and experience. That is, both thought and experience influence, are influenced by, and adapt to stimuli found in specific environments.
Within this general framework, we must note that it is the totality of life
experiences, shaped by habits, beliefs, locality, and expectations, that creates
the fertile landscape on which humans blend their broad range of experiences
with cognition to form a harmonized whole.

While some suggested that Dewey's work on the relationship between
art and the lived experiences of individuals was an abrupt departure from his

intellectual trajectory, when we see art as one important and perhaps unique aspect of human experience, it is not difficult to couch his thoughts on aesthetics within his broader work. Although Dewey had casually explored his thoughts on aesthetics in one chapter of *Experience and Nature* (Dewey, 1994), his first and only full treatment of aesthetics was *Art as Experience* (Dewey, 1934a), a work based on a series of lectures given by James in 1931. Building on James's work as well as his own belief in the importance of creating synthesis between the worlds of fact and thought, Dewey delved into the joined and harmonized relationship between art and commonplace experiences. Indeed, Dewey sought to forge a unified system, absent from dualistic structures, that was built on qualitative immediacy, harmonizing of meanings in the "consummatory phase" and the re-adaption of meaning within new and expanded understandings of the human condition. Within this framework, Dewey subtly reworked the Kantian notion of change that was based on dualistic and indeed contradictory tensions. While for Kant, change emanated from the antagonism of systems that required an affirmation, negation, and re-affirmation, Dewey fashioned a synthetic model of change that provided clear and consistent possibilities for human development within social and natural systems.

More specifically, in *Art as Experience*, Dewey adapted his naturalistic philosophy to a Hegelian system of rationality to contend that a perversion of aesthetics had occurred whereby works of art were separated from human experience, the very locus that allows art to exist. Perhaps more importantly, Dewey (1934a) suggested that so extensive and pervasive are the cleaving off of art from the real that art seems alien to most individuals. This is true, in essence, because a real aesthetic experience is one that stems from a connection of art to the experiences of everyday life. Indeed, when art is closely aligned with the products of one's vocation, the appreciation of the art work is most intense and satisfying. By contrast, when divorced from the everyday, art is cheapened and meaningless to the great mass of people.

Dewey contended that traditional aesthetic theories isolate and disconnect art from everyday life. Indeed, only in finding, or recognizing self, as a "live creature" situated within the ordinary and real of the everyday can we hope to expand and understand past experiences as well as benefit from future potentials. Although consistent with Dewey's overall philosophy his conceptualization of the role of art and aesthetics in education suffers from a teleological imperative that seems to promote human potential within a narrowly defined frame. By insisting on an ecological connection between thought, experience, and growth, Dewey sought re-harmonization based on previous understandings of self within communities. While change can, and does occur in these contexts, the possibilities for human growth are constrained within pre-existing boundaries. Further, they are dependent upon representations of art that imitates daily life and therefore appeals to the viewer. While Dewey seems to suggest a rather direct line between art and its effects upon viewers, the efficacy of this approach had been problematized as early as the late 18th century, when Jean-Jacques Rousseau, in his Letter on the spectator d'Alembert on the Theatre (1758), questioned the influence or mimetic performance on individuals. Indeed, Rousseau's criticism, much like Plato's opposition of the ethical immediacy of the chorus to the passivity of the theatre, rested on supposed but non-existent unity between performers, text, and audience.

So, while Dewey's voice often leads conversations about educational aesthetics, his views, couched as they are within pragmatic philosophy, focus on a narrowly defined pedagogy of place that while potent, is nonetheless limited by the paucity of input and the existence of environmental factors which can be pernicious and persistent detractors within some communities. We are left, then, with one final vocal addition to the conversation. Today, one of the more provocative contemporary philosophers who treats aesthetics is Jacques Rancière. While it would be essay to cordon off his thoughts on education to The Ignorant School Master: Five Lessons in Intellectual Emancipation (Rancière, 1991, hereafter Five Lessons), to do so would to be to miss important connections between his political and pedagogical work. Much like Jean-Jacques Rousseau's Emile, Five Lessons is an extension of Rancière's general philosophy as it relates to the aesthetic encounter, a fully pregnant moment that lends itself to problematizing questions of equality and visibility, and more specifically, new ways of seeing and being seen (Means, 2010).

Of course, for Rancière and others, such as Hannah Arendt, these new ways of seeing and being are political by nature because they call for revolution, whether individual or within communities. It is here that Rancière suggests that dissensus, or those moments where questioning, whether of self or police-imposed perceptions, can abound, represents an aesthetic counter to the taken-for-granted and imposed understandings of self and place that reinforce the reproductive imperative of contemporary education.

While much of his work in derived from Friedrich von Schiller's Letters on the Aesthetic Education of Man—a work in which Schiller criticizes the ways in the rise of the state, by which he potentially means politics, has cleaved the relationship between reason and sense—Rancière also avails himself to the long and rich tradition of French literature for metaphors that inform and express his thoughts. From a Stéphane Mallarmé prose-poem in particular. Rancière takes the phrase "Séparés, on est ensemble" (translated as apart, we are together) as a point of departure for discussing and constructing the aesthetic place, or the locus of solitary contemplation that is at once both separate from and connected to. While Rancière concentrates much of his discussion on politics and the question communities, there are clear implications for educational aesthetics. Separated, or what we might equally call DIS-placed curricula have, at their core, the creation of a universal educational focus that ignores the margins, excludes differences, and denies heterogeneity. The homogeneity inherent in this curriculum ignores the "séparés (separated) part of the phrase while privileging "on est ensemble" (we are together and the same).

In Rancière's account of Mallarmé's prose-poem, there is an intimate connection between separation and community. While at first glance, solitude and community might appear paradoxical, there is nonetheless a shared link between the sensory perceptions of individuals that create communities of sense, bound by and woven from the tensions of assimilation and accommodation. By now, the connections to the familiar Kantian process of change through understanding of current states, disarticulating perception, and reconfiguring new perceptions is clear. And indeed, while Rancière's work is intimately influenced by Schiller and Althusser, he nonetheless labors within the Kantian system that focuses on a relationship between subjective experiences and transcendental categories of the mind to include everyday experiences and change within social spheres. While certainly not a pragmatist like Peirce, James, or Dewey, there is nonetheless a quality of action and consequences that pervade his work.

Although an admittedly truncated genealogy of aesthetics, the foregoing discussion serves to illustrate the importance of aesthetics as both a philosophical category and an educational imperative. Although the field had to wait almost 2000 years to be named aesthetics, the early Greeks saw important connections between art, concepts of beauty, and pedagogy. Plato, for his part, saw an inherent power in art to both corrupt and instruct. *The Republic* represents Plato's fullest treatment of art and suggests, rather forcefully, that individuals and states should be governed by reason. To achieve this idyllic regime, Plato advances that education, both physical and intellectual, be a part of learning. Yet, he is also equally careful to separate "good art," by which he seemingly means works that are morally appropriate from "bad art," characterized as irrational works that emanate from sensitivity, genius, and divine inspiration (Richter, 1967). From these origins, European philosophers from the Age of Enlightenment not only named the field, but also made significant advancements, especially in the epistemology of aesthetics. Working from deference to the rational but with an understanding of the emotive potential of art, Baumgarten, Kant, Hegel, and others wove together a scientific understanding of aesthetics that remains influential even 200 years hence. Although the work of these men turned aesthetics from a pedagogical stance to a purely philosophical search for understanding the nature of knowledge, John Dewey and later Jacques Rancière refocused aesthetics on education. Each, in their own way, worked within what Rancière terms the "partage du sensible" to find the localized space, a pedagogy of place, to consider current states and to find a path toward a better understanding of the possible.

From what we have seen, art and the philosophical tradition of aesthetics are closely intertwined. For a long time, aesthetics has been largely and conventionally associated with questions of beauty and, in education, how pieces of art serve as portals to a higher level of consciousness. Morris Weitz (1972), perhaps, expressed it best in his 1971 aesthetic education lecture to the American Educational Theatre Association in Chicago. Summing up, Weitz noted the power of aesthetics to promote the full growth of children, meaning a convergence of the intellectual and the aesthetic. All accomplished, of course, through the arts broadly defined.

Today, we wish to disrupt the continuing insistence that an aesthetic education is primarily centered on the relationship between an individual and the art used for educational purposes. Indeed, as Monroe Beardsley's (1973) suggested, aesthetics should be seen as the "fulfillment that comes from awareness of the ways elements of experience interrelate in order to bring about the formation of complex unities that are marked by emergent" and new conceptualizations (p. 49). From this, we can understand that aesthetic contemplation, or what we prefer to call the aesthetic moment, represents "concepts and terms of analysis, a categorical framework, which, if freed from confinement in the autonomous aesthetic domain, would open the possibility of encountering a secular world empowered as a source of meaning beyond the self or subject" (Bernstein, 1992, p. 9). Beginning to think of aesthetics within these parameters requires a new approach to educational aesthetics that fully realizes the autonomy of the field and its ability to work on the margins to not only demonstrate how exclusions and alienation occur but also to promote strategies that recover an aesthetic education as the vehicle to combat DIS-placed curricula.

Perhaps in more simple terms and in conclusion, aesthetics should permeate all aspects of education while serving as the corrective lens that refocuses pedagogy within a localized community. At the same time, an aesthetic education, built on connections to communities and to individuals, can become a powerful pedagogical force that forges and forces the aesthetic moment—the precise point in time where the tension between the known and the unknown, the habitual and the new, as well as the comfortable and the unnerving creates a precipice on which the individual is poised to step into an abyss from which a new self will arise. The aesthetic moment in curriculum is RE-placed within a pedagogy of place and space that takes into account the means by which critical thinking, habits of mind, and self-realization can occur via a curriculum that is place-centered and which attends to the importance of locality and critical narratives within lived experience.

· 3 ·

DISRUPTING OUR IMAGINED COMMUNITIES

The Role of Ritual in Promoting Cosmopolitan Curriculum Communities

A Cosmopolitan Encounter: Museo Nacional de Antropología

Nearly a decade ago one of us traveled to Mexico City for the American Educational Studies Association annual conference and visited the Museo Nacional de Antropología, the National Museum of Anthropology after hearing that the museum held amazing artifacts spanning the indigenous cultures of Mexico. Each room in the museum houses artifacts from a specific anthropological period including, among others, formative Mesoamerica, Mexica/Aztec, Teotihuacan, and Mayan. The museum artifacts include the well-known Piedra del Sol, the Aztec Calendar Stone. The following is a personal account of those experiences:

I went to the museum with a clear agenda. I was in search of artifacts that "punctuate the stream of living" (Dewey, 1934a, p. 7). In *Art as Experience*, Dewey distinguished between the manner in which many of his time separated art from life—putting it on a pedestal or in museums. In contrast, he noted how many in ancient times took such care to create their everyday tools as objects of beauty:

Domestic utensils, furnishings of tent and house, rugs, mats, jars, pots, bows, and spears were wrought with such delighted care that today we hunt them out and give them places of honor in art museums. Yet in their own time and place, such things were enhancements of the process of everyday life instead of being elevated to a niche apart, they belonged to display of prowess, the manifestations of group and clan membership, worship of gods, feasting and fasting, fighting, hunting, and all the rhythmic crises that punctuate the stream of living (pp. 6–7).

I wanted to see these works of art that ancient communities used in their everyday lives: jars, bowls, combs, and the like. As I entered each room, I immediately encountered the larger artifacts—statues, remnants of mosaics depicting warfare, religious symbols, etc. I had to seek out the smaller displays often housed in the back corners of the rooms. It was in these smaller display cases that I would find beautiful treasures: a water jug used to carry water from a communal well, an ornately carved comb I imagined ancient mothers using on their children's hair, cooking utensils, and jewelry. Era after era I found these everyday objects displayed. Each encounter gave me pause—seeing those objects impressed upon me how I was connected to those ancient women. By the time I was ready to leave the museum, I was overwhelmed by a sense of connection, by the existential reality that I am a historical being—shaped even by these women who came hundreds of years before.

When I first entered the museum that day, I saw a colleague across the room. He too had come to the museum alone that day. We waved to one another and proceeded with our independent journeys through the museum. Later that evening, I saw the colleague at a reception. I asked him what he thought of the museum. His reaction was visceral. Despondent, he talked about how disturbed he had been in the museum. He struggled with how we can come from such violent civilizations, and he wondered, after seeing so many artifacts depicting violence and war, if there was hope for peace in the future. Upon hearing of his experience, I then shared my own. I told him that I left the museum full of hope. Instead of lingering over the images of warfare, I sought out images of family, community, and connection. I then told him about the water jugs, the combs, and the jewelry hidden in the smaller displays in each room. Following our conversation, I would catch glimpses of my colleague during the reception. He was thinking and still struggling with his experiences from the day. As the evening wore on, my colleague came back to me with a determined look: "I'm going to go back to the museum," he announced, "I want to see what you saw."

Ours were cosmopolitan encounters. Cosmopolitanism involves connec-tions—being in relationship with others, even when those connections span hundreds of years. To achieve a cosmopolitan state of being, we must embrace both kinds of experiences: welcoming the awe of all that is good around us as well as recognizing our relationship with pain, suffering, and evil itself. With this in mind, I explore the significance of cosmopolitanism as it relates to cur-riculum and argue that we cannot sustain a cosmopolitan curriculum without clear means to shift from the abstract to the concrete and without further means to help us sustain the disturbed sense of self we must have in order to stay in authentic relationships with one another. For this to happen, we must rely on ritual.

Cosmopolitanism

As noted in chapter one, references to community when addressing curric-ulum fall short because our trajectory of action mindset in curriculum work promotes, at best, interaction, not transaction. Further, the accountability narrative that pervades educators' work exacerbates this phenomenon. As a result, the kinds of communities we create within schools and universities are, at best, imagined communities (Anderson, 2006). We imagine the students as objects through which we build our global economy, and we base our curric-ulum decisions on these assumptions and images. Foster (2002) concurs. He argues that the nature of schooling has been formed by "an increasing and now global network of administrative control over schools and the educational process" (p. 6). While Foster argues that we should counteract the economic forces by shifting our images of schools from organizations to communities, his recommendations still leave room for the kinds of interactional dynamics that currently exist. As Talbert and Boyles (2005) argue, simply shifting how we organize and talk about schooling from the larger bureaucratic system to a "community" does not guarantee that we rid the system of its impersonality and prevent the curriculum from objectifying students and teachers. Such a shift may simply offer a smaller scale of impersonal, bureaucratic operation that continues to disengage those involved.

In order to promote the kind of transactional work needed to promote growth and meaning making, we need to ensure that the communities we achieve in schools and universities are cosmopolitan communities (Appiah, 2006; Hansen, 2010; Pinar, 2009; Nussbaum, 1997). We need to find ways in which we can balance the student as a "being half hidden in a cloud of unknowing" (Huebner, 1999/1975, p. 219) with the larger social aims of a democratic society.

Cosmopolitanism is the opposite of what we see in Hogarth's *Gin Lane* described in a previous chapter. Cosmopolitanism involves living in relationship with the world and recognizing the opportunity that relationship, however painful it might be at times, provides for living more authentic lives and building more just communities. We encounter existentially unique others, and we see those encounters as opportunities to become more aware of our world and ourselves. Because of this awareness of our relationship with others, we achieve greater authenticity. Each encounter invites us to become better people. Through this process, we recognize how we are more than the sum of our parts—that our shared normative project: seeking truth, beauty, and justice (elements of a liquid modernity as Bauman [2000] describes) impacts our community now and in the future. We are part of one body—transcending geography, culture, history, and ideology. In order to work toward cosmopolitan possibilities, we have to develop the capacity to accept within this body the pain and complexity of others. This requires developing, acknowledging, and sustaining a disturbed sense of self. Sennett (1994) describes the audacity of such efforts:

> This can only occur, I believe, by understanding why bodily pain requires a place in which it can be acknowledged, and in which its transcendent origins become visible. Such a pain has a trajectory in human experience... the body accepting of pain is ready to become a civic body... But the body can follow this civic trajectory only if it acknowledges that there is no remedy for its sufferings in the contrivings of society, that its unhappiness has come from elsewhere, that is pain derives from God's command to live together as exiles (p. 376).

It is only in and because of this awareness that we can approximate cosmopolitan ideals. According to Delaney (2006), critical cosmopolitanism occurs "whenever new relations between self, other, and world develop in moments of openness" (p. 27). It resides in social mechanisms and dynamics of any place and time in which we are open to possibilities that may arise from our differences. Critical cosmopolitanism involves social and self-transformation emerging from new spaces for complicated conversations. He notes, "The cosmopolitan imagination from the perspective of critical social theory of modernity tries to capture the transformative moment, interactive relations between societies and modernities, the developmental and dialogic"

(Delaney, 2006, p. 44). Through a cosmopolitan effort, we work together as vulnerable and unfinished beings. We hold onto our existential selves, acknowledging both the sacred and the profane, while we simultaneously let go of ourselves and accept that we are part of this larger civic body. Only then can we engage in authentic complicated conversations: conversation where we are not projecting, we are not trying to convert or convince. Instead, we are trying to connect, to question, and to understand. It is through this passage between the subjective and the social (Pinar, 2009) that we journey together through an abyss of unknowing. As Hansen (2009) notes, we are all intersubjective social beings. We are more than the culmination of the social and psychological forces that impact us.

We must transcend the everyday pressures of seeing everything as a means to an end—of seeing others as means to ends. As Pinar (2009) laments, "Stripped of its meaning, experience has been reduced to a means to an end" (p. ix). When we are in relationship with one another, we do not see others as objects of utility. If we can transcend these pressures, then cosmopolitan inheritance is within our grasp: convictions, values, ideas, practices, hopes, and yearnings (Hansen, 2009) to enrich the quality of our shared lived experiences. Ek and Mcintyre Latta (2013) recognize this challenge as a nexus wherein we continually seek our epistemological/ontological bearings. They note, "Such a mediating ground attends to understanding what each encounter conveys... It assumes learning be brought into being, concomitantly bringing self into being, too" (Ek & Mcintyre Latta, 2013, p. 97). Cosmopolitanism necessitates this constant state of courageous vulnerability and productive tension (Hansen, 2009) wherein we seek the disruptions and tensions so that we may protect ourselves from complacency and live more authentically with one another. As noted in a previous chapter, it is not only that willingness to offer the helpful gaze to the junkie on the train and to be constantly open to extending that gaze, but it also involves seeing ourselves in the eyes of the junkie and recognizing how we are all part of one body, and as such shape the conditions within which the junkie live and are shaped by the world the junkie helps to create.

Curriculum and Cosmopolitanism

When we work toward a cosmopolitan curriculum, we must first begin with the student as the subjective starting point of our complicated conversations and our curricular deliberations. We consider the student in relation to his or her being-in-the-world as an existential and active agent within the world while we also recognize that he or she is part of the larger civic body (Pinar, 2009; Sennett, 1994). With this in mind, we must acknowledge that we begin our conversations and deliberations aware of the tensions between individual identities and our lives as collective subjects. As Pinar (2009) notes, "As epiphenomenal, identity both enables and constrains our capacity to articulate and thereby reconstruct our being-in-the-world" (loc. 925).

Therefore, we begin with the individual, but we do so within a complicated social context. As Dewey noted in My Pedagogic Creed (1897),

> I believe that the only true education comes through the stimulation of the child's powers by the demands of the social situations in which he finds himself. Through these demands he is stimulated to act as a member of a unity, to emerge from his original narrowness of action and feeling and to conceive of himself from the standpoint of the welfare of the group to which he belongs (p. 78).

Thus, we cannot talk about curriculum without considering it within the context of a community. Curriculum exists by virtue of assumptions regarding those who will be impacted by it. Curriculum invokes a complicated conversation that demands not only a community but also a cosmopolitan imagination. We must be poised to engage with the world and with one another. In order to do this, we must recognize five key elements of a cosmopolitan curriculum identified by Pinar (2009).

First, cosmopolitan curriculum is complex. According to Pinar (2009), it juxtaposes the abstract and the concrete, the collective and the individual, history and biography, politics and art, public service and private passion. All of these elements of being-in-the-world must be encountered through moments of openness. Delanty (2006) notes, "Critical cosmopolitanism is an open process by which the social world is made intelligible; it should be seen as the expression of new ideas, opening spaces of discourse, identifying possibilities for translation, and the construction of the social world" (p. 42). It is our moral obligation to create spaces in which these elements of being-in-the-world can be acknowledged and where students can grapple with the tensions inherent in these complexities not only for themselves but also for society.

Second, cosmopolitan curriculum is social. While it is important to help students to learn to think for themselves and to build their capacity for imagination and growth, we must also help students to recognize that they think for themselves so that they can work toward a more just world. Authenticity cannot exist in isolation. Further, authenticity cannot be fully realized in an unjust world. As Ayers (2013) contends, "All children need to develop a sense of unique capacity of human beings to shape and create reality in concert with conscious purposes and plans" (p. 133). Hansen (2009) refers to this aim as developing students as intersubjective social beings. Work toward social justice reciprocates in kind. By being in the world and seeking more authentic shared lives in the world, we achieve deeper levels of authenticity personally. Pinar (2009) concurs: "Passionate lives subjectively expressed through public service invite self-understanding through self-overcoming" (loc. 162).

Third, cosmopolitan curriculum is historical. We need to approach our curriculum conversations and deliberations with Heidegger's (1962) "ecstatic temporality." We have been. We are. We will be. While these statements on the page are separated by conventional punctuation, these three aspects of who we are cannot be separated. As such, we exist as temporal beings. We do not focus on the present nor do we focus on a predetermined and thus controlled future. Instead, we are poised for the infinite possibilities the future holds with full awareness that our past and our present influence those possibilities. This relationship between the past, present, and future is not an individual journey. As Huebner (1986) notes, it is part of an individual-world dialectic:

> The springs or sources of temporality do not reside in the individual, but in conjunction between the individual and other individuals... Thus man shapes the world, but the world also shapes the man. This is the dialectic process in which cause is effect, and effect is cause. The world calls forth new responses from the individual, who in turn calls forth new responses from the world (p. 328).

A cosmopolitan curriculum must create spaces where the past, present, and future may dwell simultaneously and where students can wrestle with their personal biographies alongside their shared histories (Huebner, 1987; Pinar, 2011).

Fourth, a cosmopolitan curriculum is reflective (Ek & Macintyre Latta, 2013). It requires nurturing a sincere desire to engage reflexively in the shared learning experience (Dewey, 1938). Pinar (2009) suggests that a cosmopolitan education invites self-reflection and notes that while this self-reflection is often associated with solitude, we must do so while engaged with others. Together we approach the experience open to possibilities and anticipate that the experience will change us—both individually and collectively. It is through this anticipation of change that we achieve a sense of agency.

This process is on-going. Hansen et al. (2010) note that this anticipation of change is not limited to one encounter. A cosmopolitan curriculum presumes continual change. Further, this continual reflective process in relation with others—this dialogic process—thrives on difference. We do not engage in this dialogic process in order to solve a problem. We enter into engaged reflection with others so that who we are in the world is enlarged by who we are together (Hansen, 2009).

Finally, a cosmopolitan curriculum is lived. Who we are and what we will become is a result of how we engage with our lived experiences and the degree to which we ensure that those experiences are educative. Through those lived experiences, we build a normative and discursive world together. We erect "intellectual and lived bridges between self and society" (Pinar, 2009, p. 27). By engaging with one another temporally, fully awake, and poised for possibilities, we achieve *currere*: thriving on difference and allowing it to draw us out of ourselves and more fully immersed in the world so that we may seek justice in the world. (Hansen, 2008; Pinar, 2009). So much of what is happening in schools today expends tremendous effort to suppress the lived experiences of students. Standardization and identity politics in schools impose dark clouds over students' experiences through which little light can escape (Pinar, 2009) and educators respond with ideologically vapid "solutions" or theories removed from material reality (Au, 2012). Thus, as we begin our curriculum deliberations and ask ourselves, "What knowledge is of most worth?" we need to understand the magnitude of this question and the moral implications of our response. Further, we need to recognize that we are deliberating about worth at this time and in this particular place because our lived experiences are continually changing. For this reason we ask the question while considering both the concrete lived experience and the abstract being in time. Our response to that question can never be objectified nor can it be dismissed by accusations of essentializing philosophically complex phenomena. By virtue of our moral calling as educators, we are compelled to approximate cosmopolitan ideals in our curriculum deliberations.

How can we approximate cosmopolitan ideals within our curriculum work? We can begin with reverence (Rud & Garrison, 2013). Reverence involves an understanding of human limitations and imperfections. It requires a sense of awe alongside feelings of respect, shame, and humility. We enter into reverent relationships knowing that we are not in control, but we are nevertheless agents in our shared lived experiences. Consider again the mother on the train in Audre Lorde's (1972/1992) poem mentioned before. Her response was a reverent act. She recognized the existential moment, the unique place and time that brought her and the girl "with a horse in her brain" together on the train. Along that continuum of time and space, fate would bring that girl to slump down beside her. The woman recognizes her place in this lived experience: "Little girl/ on the nod/ if we are measured by dreams we avoid/ then you are the nightmare/ of all sleeping mothers." This is a moment in which shame, respect, and humility reside together. And yet, that acknowledgement alone is not reverent, for reverence requires action: the woman reaches out to help. Knowing that she did not have control over the situation, the woman nevertheless offered compassion to the stranger on the train because she saw how they were connected and wanted to bring concrete meaning to that connection. Similarly, when we strive to create and sustain a cosmopolitan curriculum we attempt to make the abstract connections concrete and present. Like the woman, we may be met with rejection, but we must have faith and conviction sufficient to continue trying.

An Approximation of Cosmopolitan Curriculum: Oakland Cemetery

A few years ago I had the opportunity to teach a course on postmodern curriculum theorizing to a group of doctoral students in Atlanta. I wrestled with the typical confines of a doctoral seminar where students read preordained texts and then discuss them, recognizing the challenge of engaging students in authentic conversations within the confines of a traditional institution that measures everything with traditional grades. Regardless of how "safe" I tried to create the space, the fact remained that as the professor in the class, I held the power and to some degree their engagement would be couched in a need for my approval. In an attempt to disrupt the traditional spaces of the academy, I organized the course around curricular spaces: aesthetic, commodified, violent, historical, etc. We then worked together to identify spaces in the city where we could encounter shared lived experiences.

On the evening where we were exploring historical spaces, we met at Oakland Cemetery, a cemetery in the heart of the city that was built in 1850 and serves as the final resting place for many citizens in the city's history, both notable and unnamed. My only "instructions" for the evening were to go and experience the space. After two hours in the cemetery, we met at the pub across the street, aptly named "Six Feet Under," and discussed what we experienced. The conversation was animated. Students discussed their reactions to the divisions created within the cemetery—deteriorating walls that separated people based upon their religion and social class. They discussed the tombstones they saw for babies without names and how families in the past could bury an infant without a name—what that meant during a time when death was so commonplace. They discussed their mixed emotions regarding the large open field where many of the city's indigents were buried in large, unmarked graves. They were conflicted about whether they were comforted or offended at the thought that families across generations frolicked across and picnicked on those fields. After discussing their initial experiences in the space, they began to juxtapose the abstract with the concrete (Pinar, 2009). They considered the work of Freire when he notes that we are all historical beings, and they began to consider how they were connected to and shaped by those who were buried in the cemetery—both individually and collectively. At some level it was easy to imagine the connection: thoughts of family and legacy. Yet, they struggled with the possibility that they were shaped by the same forces that created the physical barriers in that space. What did it mean to be part of a community, like so many others, where discrimination was such a strong part of its history? How did those images of difference shape them individually and collectively?

The Role of Ritual in Promoting a Cosmopolitan Curriculum

Ideology alone cannot create or sustain a cosmopolitan curriculum. We need a mechanism through which we can juxtapose the abstract with the concrete. Ritual offers promise to create the spaces in which we can attach meaning to our actions and feel connected to one another. According to Marshall (2002), ritual brings about a sense of belonging. Sennett concurs (2003). He notes that rituals bring common actions into a communal setting; they help us orient ourselves to one another. Marshall (2002) identifies a critical element within rituals that is consistent with cosmopolitanism: co-presence. He notes that when individuals are faced with ambiguity in their lives, they look to one another to find security, validation, and reassurance. Not only does co-presence help individuals feel connected to one another, it also promotes a shift from self-centeredness. Individuals engaging in rituals lose a sense of themselves as they feel connected to those with whom they are sharing the experience.

Ritual also brings about greater levels of understanding. Marshall (2002) points to extensive research indicating that people, for the most part, act mindlessly or automatically under the control of social and emotional forces of which they are unaware. Rituals, by virtue of being effortful and shared, allow individuals to attach meaning to their actions, making the subject of the ritual important and meaningful. Further, Marshall argues that rituals force individuals to seek coherence in their overall practices. He notes, "When actuating reasons are ambiguous or transparent and no obvious external justification presents itself, we are forced to change our internal cognitions and beliefs in order to maintain a sense of consistency and reduce our aversive state of dissonance" (Marshall, 2002, p. 368).

Jennings (1982) goes further in exploring the noetic functions of ritual. First, he notes that ritual action provides a way to gain knowledge—a means to inquiry and discovery. He points to historical and cultural studies of ritual demonstrating that what on the surface may appear to be identical rituals actually include variations that indicate they are more than mere repetition. Thus he concludes, "Ritual knowledge is gained through a bodily action which alters the world or the place of the ritual participant in the world... It is primarily corporeal rather than cerebral, primarily active rather than contemplative, primarily transformative rather than speculative" (Jennings, 1982, p. 112). He argues that ritual action does not merely invite imitation; it invokes response, and the response is not controlled or dictated by the ritual. While the pattern of action within a ritual is governed by the structure and nature of the ritual, the act itself is a "minded action" within which the participant is fully conscious. Jennings notes that ritual knowledge is gained through action. It forms an embodied knowing within the act itself—not as a precursor to the act or as a reflection following it.

Second, Jennings (1982) notes that rituals serve a pedagogical role by transmitting knowledge. He contends that rituals not only teach participants to see differently, they also teach them to act differently. Rather than offering a point of view, rituals offer patterns of action through response. While the response may be provoked and patterned after the ritual, it is not controlled or dictated by the action. Further, the response can then be applied to situations outside the parameters of the ritual itself. Therefore, in addition to teaching individuals how to conduct themselves within a ritual, the ritual also teaches them how to conduct themselves outside of the ritual. Jennings (1982) offers the Lord's Prayer as an example—noting that it may serve as a model for all prayerful acts. As such, Jennings contends, "Ritual serves as a paradigm for all significant action" (p. 118).

Finally, Jennings notes that ritual knowledge is gained by virtue of the ritual serving as an object of knowledge itself. Inherent within any ritual act is the notion of an audience or a spectator—whether that audience is literal or ideal. Ritual involves those engaged making themselves known to others and inviting others to participate. What is known from this engagement is knowledge gained, transmitted, and received in action. In this manner, according to Jennings, ritual knowledge is not only distinct *from* reflective knowledge, it is also the starting point *for* reflective knowledge. Thus, not only does ritual invite participants to inquire, the inquiry becomes an extension of that ritual. Rituals are therefore designed to be translated and relevance regarding its relation to life outside of itself becomes part of the translation.

Given the social and intellectual benefits of ritual outlined by Marshall and Jennings, we can explore their potential for creating and sustaining a cosmopolitan curriculum. As Dewey (1916) notes that we live in a community to the degree that we have something in common. Ideas often fail to form common links when they are shared among individuals who have very different motivations as well as degrees of engagement, confidence, and competence. Rituals, on the other hand, create common bonds among diverse people; they are common actions within a communal setting. Furthermore, rituals allow participants to transform something material into something expressive, and the object of that expression is shared (Sennett, 2004). Thus, a community brought together by ritual can achieve mutuality when they do not possess equality—when their commitment, competence, or confidence may not be the same.

Consider, for example, the pagan rituals adopted within Christian celebrations of various holidays. Symbols such as a Christmas tree, Santa Claus, and the like are rooted in pagan celebrations, but Christians worldwide recognize and use them as part of their celebrations. Individuals hold these symbols in varied levels of esteem, and some may approach them with more deliberate religious intentions while others focus on the secular elements of the holidays. Nevertheless, these symbols and rituals bind those who celebrate the season. Thus, considering Dewey's (1927) notion of community, rituals can serve as instrumentalities through which we can create and support cosmopolitan dispositions within their schools:

> Wherever there is conjoint activity whose consequences are appreciated as good by all singular persons who take part in it, and where the realization of the good is such as to effect an energetic desire and effort to sustain it in being just because it is a good shared by all, there is in so far a community (p. 149).

Rituals for a Cosmopolitan Curriculum

Nearly two decades ago, Neil Postman (1995) argued that in order for schools to make sense, students, parents, and teachers needed to have a god or gods to serve. He argued that "there is no surer way to bring about an end to schooling than for it to have no end" (Postman, 1995, p. 4). For Postman, gods became the narrative that brought meaning and purpose to schools. Yet, as I ponder Postman's challenge, I cannot help but think about the golden calf the Israelites made to worship Baal as they waited for Moses to return from the mountaintop. In spite of the miracles they witnessed while they were delivered from Egypt, "God," or the idea of a god was not enough to sustain them. This is not to say that a sense of purpose, a god or series of gods, is not important. It is. However, a narrative or idea or mission in and of itself is insufficient. Something more is needed in order to achieve and sustain a cosmopolitan curriculum. With this in mind, I offer the following rituals as mere suggestions:

Ritual Giving

We can see a number of examples of rituals that involve bestowing gifts on others. The tradition has certainly made its way into a number of holiday celebrations as well as other notable points in one's life (birth, confirmation, marriage, etc.). Sennett (2004) offers another of the ritual of giving is offered with the Trobrianders of New Guinea. Members of this tribe were bound together by the ritual of giving and receiving necklaces and bracelets during a market festival. In this ritual, individuals offer gifts to others—humbly throwing the necklaces or bracelets at the feet of the receiver. Similarly, the receiver responds with humility—acting as if he or she cannot accept it. By giving away the jewelry, the man in this tribe obligates others to do the same. The ritual binds all members of the community. Because people's resources were unequal, the exchanges were, according to Sennett, asymmetrical. Differences were accepted as part of the exchange. The rite itself bound them in spite of the differences of their socioeconomic status.

How might this ritual giving relate to curriculum? To the degree that we can create conditions in which asymmetrical giving among professionals, we can create a mutual vulnerability that will support a community of inquiry. More importantly, the ritual act of giving obligates all members of the community to reciprocal exchange. As Dewey (1916) notes, this relationship changes all involved by enlarging their collective experience. He describes this relationship as follows:

> The desired transformation is not difficult to define in a formal way. It signifies a society in which every person shall be occupied in something which makes the lives of others more perceptible—which breaks down the barriers of distance between them (p. 316).

Ritual Dance

According to Durkheim (2001), the most characteristic feature of positive rites is rhythmic movement. Marrett (1914) concurs. He notes that "Savage religion is not so much thought out as danced out" (p. xxxi). Marshall (2002) notes that rhythmic movement creates both belonging and effervescence. As such, dance lets the participant escape from him or herself. It affects the emotional state and creates a common emotional experience. For the most part, dance serves no other purpose. It has no inherent extrinsic value. It may produce enjoyment, but otherwise individuals engaging in dance do so for its own sake. With this in mind, I would challenge us to consider traditions, exercises, and general practices that we could initiate within our schools that have no explicit extrinsic value—particularly value when attached to accountability and testing. It is only in this open space of engagement that substantive inquiry and thus meaningful community will emerge. As Dewey (1927) notes,

> To be able to get away for a time from entanglement in the urgencies and needs of immediate practical concerns is a condition of the origin of scientific treatment in any field. Preoccupation with attaining some direct end or practical utility always limits scientific inquiry (pp. 16–17).

Ritual Meals

Meals are a part of a number of rituals across cultures and time. From Thanksgiving dinner to a Passover Seder or a Eucharistic feast, people come together with food. They join in a community that extends far beyond the confines of a family home, synagogue, or cathedral. Ritual meals are historical. As I have grown into an adult, I recall images of Thanksgivings from my childhood, sitting in small chairs and hovering over a wobbly coffee table while the adults ate at the big table. I remember spying everyone's "favorites" that my aunts dutifully prepared each year to demonstrate how special each family member was. And as I got older I saw myself taking on more and more of the responsibilities for the feast, particularly as those same aunts succumbed to advanced years and Alzheimer's. I now make sure I prepare those special dishes that I know they love and can no longer make. As family mebers die and others are born, the traditions continue—much of what makes the meal a ritual is rooted in those traditions from family members now gone. In addition to Thanksgiving meals and Passover Seders held in homes among family and friends, other ritual meals draw more disparate members of a community together.

The Eucharistic feast brings together a community to share in bread and wine symbolizing the body and blood of Jesus. This ritual takes place in varied forms across many denominations and over hundreds of years. While some churches restrict who may commune based upon age, denomination, or marital status, the image of the Eucharist nevertheless creates the possibility for individuals holding very different views and living very different lives to come together and have an experience that is simultaneously individual and communal, present and historical, spiritual and political. Each person comes to the altar by choice and is often joined by strangers. The prophet and the whore may kneel side-by-side and extend their hands for the bread. The priest does not stop to ask their motivation, convictions, or levels of devotion. Rather, the bread and the wine are freely given, and each recipient responds to the gift in his or her unique way. Some may merely seek consistency of habit while others may seek redemption and transformation. The possibilities following accepting the bread and wine are open.

Ritual meals remind us of the importance of connections. They remind us that we are members of a larger global and historical community and when we humble ourselves together at the altar, we embrace who we are individually as well as who we are as part of the larger body. As the Eucharist binds us across time and place, so does our cosmopolitan community. The differences we possess are the very substance needed for the complicated curriculum conversations.

Conclusion

In this era of accountability, we face tremendous challenges in our attempts to disrupt the imagined communities found within our schools and universities. We must be diligent to identify the narratives, policies, and practices that promote interactions instead of transactions. Scholars such as Pinar (2009) and Hansen (2010) have articulated images of cosmopolitan ideals for schools that can support transactional communities. Yet, ideological images are often elusive in education. We struggle with enacting ideals through our policies and daily practices. To this end, rituals such as those suggested here offer a means through which we can achieve the cosmopolitan curriculum we so desperately need in schools today.

· 4 ·

RE-ASSESSING AND RE-CAPTURING SPACE THROUGH RADICAL CURRICULUM

In his autobiographical sketch of life in Yazoo City, Mississippi, Willie Morris (1971) described it was normal to display proudly equality in spirituality and protest racial equality during the civil rights movement. The spirituality of individuals is in constant conflict as we are pulled violently within the spaces between our perceived needs and reality. Søren Kierkegaard believed that democracy was a key element in this dialogue. "There is a need for singular and social agency in the moment of dissent as much as we require the transgressive corrective during supposedly normal times of identity formation and democratic institutionalization" (Matustik & Westphal, 1995, p. 257). Although fragile and easily submitted to tyranny and power, democratic spaces offer an alternative toward self-liberation that allows for expression and living synchronously. Thus, democratic spaces are a key to overcome the conflict within us about finding a place, and becoming one with society.

In such an attempt, there is a need for a revolutionary self-examination in terms of thought and practice, a revolution in the Freirean (1970) sense, where open discourse helps us understand each other recovering the "mechanistic society" (Ruciman, 1978), where citizens become integral parts of a larger society, and where relationships are intimate and open. What we have proposed in this book is an attempt to understand space. In this case, it will be accomplished through considering our racial past and approach the conflict between the races through curriculum change focusing on the impact of space in urban areas. Benedict Anderson's (1991) concept of imagined communities is important to explore the concept of cultural identity as we have discussed in the book. Anderson described imagined community as *imagined* because although the members of the community might not know each other, "in the minds of each lives the image of their communion" (Anderson, 1991, p. 6). It is a *community*, because, "regardless of the actual inequality and exploitation that may prevail in each, the nation is always conceived as a deep, horizontal comradeship" (Anderson, 1991, p. 7).

Our society is concerned with place and past, especially within urban identities—and even more with racial relations within those urban spaces. The U.S., hectic in its acculturation and assimilation has never honestly dealt with the above issues in its social institutions (e.g., schools, work, etc.). As the onus of civil rights, individual racial identity was methodically placed at the forefront of U.S. culture before community equity. As a nation we have always faced problems of race, and had to invent new forms of expression from which to define the new social roles it had created—sometimes that has led to war (U.S. Civil War) and other times to social change (Second Reconstruction— civil rights movement). Louis Castenell and William Pinar (1993) write that it is an "understatement to observe that issues of race are paramount in contemporary curriculum debates in the public sphere" (Castenell & Pinar, 1993, p. 2). They suggest that curriculum is "racial text" because debates about what we teach youngsters are "debates over who we perceive ourselves to be, and how we will represent that identity, including what remains as 'left over,' as 'difference'" (Castenell & Pinar, 1993, p. 2). Curriculum as race, text and identity implies understanding the 'American national identity, and vice versa' as racial text (Castenell & Pinar, 1993, p. 2). Race and identity are terms that are constantly changing, one grows out of the individual's past, as say for example, 'black' from slavery, whereas identity comes from how the individual deals with her past, and what role society assigns that past.

Schooling is merely an institutional representation of the social milieu that encompasses it. As curriculum is nationalized and standardized it has excluded aspects of individual identity, forcing marginalization through the public policy of desegregation. Although the media tell us that we have similar needs and wants, Castenell and Pinar state that "all Americans are racialized beings; knowledge of who we have been, who we are, and who we will become is a story or text we will construct" (Castenell and Pinar, 1993,

p. 8). The focus of schooling has changed from regional to national as culture has shifted from regional to national.

Once we realize that there is a terrible conflict causing strain on our relationships and a schism of unbelievable proportions in society, we must then act. Each individual must examine her soul, then remove herself from society and conduct a critical self-examination. When this step has been taken, the individual will then be able to return to society and attempt to live out that social change. There is hope that within the school system and its curriculum there are still grey spaces where individuals can address concepts of social justice and equality. We can educate our learners in this manner, teaching them to ask critical questions. The path through curriculum must undertake a real and personal analysis of slavery. Nicholas Onuf (1989) offers a positive of creating a public knowledge basis for criticism. In his attempt to rescue the field International Relations, Onuf wished for the field to break out of the boundaries of existing disciplines (Onuf, 1989, p. 11–12). In Onuf's view, fundamental argument is conducted in the social sciences by reinterpreting classical works. This undertaking cannot be judged in absolute terms. As one makes one's way through what seems to be a random selection of texts, Onuf points to the primary characteristic of modernity, a pluralistic complexity in which competing skills and organization produce specialism and differentiation, of which the state is one such organization.

Similarly, in our zest to form counter narratives and discredit structural models of schools and curriculum, we have awakened a dangerous neoconservative response to the attack of a perceived viable model of schools accepted as legitimate (because of its accountability factor) without offering a real alternative. If as a field, curriculum designers do not heed Onuf's (1989) warning we leave ourselves without an entree to the institutions we are supposed to change.

Giddens (1976; 1991) sees the individual as an active participant in social life and not a mere bystander in search for identity. He is also critical of the poststructuralists' neglect of the structural aspects of society and their binding effects on action, and attributes self-efficacy to the individual in dealing with the search for identity. Ironically, an approach to undergird the curriculum is to erect from a deconstructionist point of view. As Derrida (1978) intended, deconstruction is the rigorous critique of the fundamental axioms of Western thought, with the purpose of exposing its biases via an analysis of the contradictions of major western philosophical texts. This process is not only negative (destruction of the axioms) but also positive (reconstruction of the axioms in a novel manner). Conceptually, the individual is removed from her societal reality, explores her I (self), then examines the Other independently. Once the two points of view have been explored, they will then become the foundation to reconstruct a new approach. As intended, the approach can have an effect as experienced by George Bailey in It's a Wonderful Life, removed and forced to see his life. One key, many times taken for granted, is the ability to communicate the experience with others. When there is truthful dialogue, when I communicate to another, the meaning I convey is what I intend to transmit to that person (Sturrock, 1979). Dialogue is essential to my story.

Curriculum links our past and future through our present. The past existed and the future will exist but the reality relies on the relation to the present. Culler (1976/1979) states that "the future is an anticipated presence and the past a former presence" (p. 162). Speech is accorded a cardinal place in Western metaphysics: logocentrism. Logocentrism asserts that speech is more authentic than writing. Speech emanates directly from the mind (the intentions of the individual) and it is thus purer and more authentic than writing. Writing contaminates speech by corrupting the authenticity of thought, which can only be transmitted unadulterated through speech (Dews, 1987, p. 10).

Derrida's view allows for a reexamination of the entire project of modern epistemology. It is possible to deconstruct the truth claims of writers by analyzing how they employ rhetorical and self-privileging strategies in the construction of their truth claims (Derrida, 1981). The implication of this quest for certainty is the search for foundations and the establishment of secure principles from which we can build a conceptual edifice that can capture the chaotic world of facts and contingencies. Derrida contends that the history of Western metaphysics (metaphysics of presence) is a constant search for foundations. As an example, Derrida (1978) suggested that

> It could be shown that all the names related to fundamentals, to principle, or to the center have always designated an invariable presence—eidos, arche, telos, energia, ousia (essence, existence, substance, subject) aletheia, transcendentality, consciousness, God, man and so forth (pp. 279–80).

The question arises of how to allow for each individual, given her past, to retain her individual experience and thus change her future.

Schools have been places where society is perpetuated, conformity taught, and deviance discouraged. Schools force children to learn the norms and values of the dominant culture; first, through emulation (most power-ful, where the child believes what she is learning is good); second, through diplomacy (where the school tries to prove to the child that school is good); third, through manipulation (by bribing the child with a diploma); fourth, by threatening force (making the child learn what is taught, ill-equipping the child for thinking) and; lastly, by force (where the child is miseducated, leading to a society of drones). This cultural hegemony can be overcome by exposing truths of life, thereby empowering the child to choose her real reali-ty, not one the school has pre-chosen for her.

Since poststructuralists have revealed "the truth" to be an outcome of power configurations (Foucault 1977, 1980), linguistically biased and arbitrary philosophical hierarchies (Derrida, 1981, 1982; Rorty, 1979), or self-referential language games (Lyotard, 1984), there is a tendency for them to conclude that modern conceptualizations of truth and reality are outmoded concepts, since both truth and reality appear to be the products of discourse, there is little need to write as if discourse must originate in them. Thus, the only viable option for theory is to recognize itself as a form of literature and practice poetics or polemics, because in the literary model, theory no lon-ger needs to defend its claim of representing the real—for the real is always brought into being by language (Rorty, 1982). It is an attempt to end the hegemonic control on truth by science.

Today, actor accounts are considered more real and truer than the con-trived and second hand conceptual schemes of traditional philosophers. The only reality is that which is constructed, interpreted and acted by human beings. Thus, it is the task of the phenomenological/hermeneutic approach to explain how everyday knowledge is created and maintained, not to assess its validity or truthfulness (Berger and Luchmann, 1967, p. 3). Incidentally, Jurgen Habermas (1990, p. 128) sheds light on the issue of individuality and communication when he synthesizes that there is a "mutual exclusivity of the various types of discourse or standards of rationality" amongst the spheres of the moral, aesthetic and scientific, that we can translate from one discourse to another, and that, through the medium of intersubjective communication it is possible to legitimize validity claims.

If we believe that "analytic thinking of modernity must be replaced by critical historicity," and that the "linear model divides time into the past, present and future, and as a result removes any autobiographical connection to the historical events" (Slattery, 1995, p. 41), then what are we searching for? Empowerment of the individual or that individual's truth? Or will finding the truth, empower the individual? Or will empowerment lead to that individual's truth? Truth is then the search for the self as well as the self-awareness that comes with genuine discovery of the I. Empowerment is the ability to recognize your awareness and harness it into participation within the larger society. In other words, take yourself out of your context, discover yourself, look at and examine society, and then place yourself within it to make a difference. We are a product of the past, and once we realize that, then we can examine our present, make corrections and change our future.

Karl Popper (1984/1992) offers an alternative position to poststructuralism. He believes that knowledge is the search for truth—"the search for objective truth" (4). His turn on the power of language is a little different from the poststructuralists. Popper is a phenomenologist, in the tradition of Hegel (Pinkard, 1994). Popper believes that for Hegel human language is descriptive statements (with self-expression and symbolism), and that we have added argumentative functions (a way to check our own theories for the objective truth). This leads to the invention of criticism, which is a conscious choice of theories over natural selection. We can find and eradicate our errors consciously. This is the first step in the beginning of human knowledge. "There is no knowledge without rational criticism, criticism is the service of the search for truth" (Popper, 1984/1992, p. 21).

Although "we can predict the future, but not well, we cannot see the unforeseeable consequences of our actions" (Popper 1984/1992, p. 28), which leads us to then address how we build a curriculum model for studying races that satisfies postmodernist thought, Tylerian accountability and individual experiences. That is up to the individual. They must follow each step. The teacher must allow for the child to learn through the questioning of the facts. Knowledge is the search for truth. There is no criterion of truth; "even when we have reached the truth we can never be certain of it. There is a rational criterion for progress in the search for truth. Science is a critical activity" (38). If we are convinced that we are in search for a truth, not a metanarrative truth, but an individual hermeneutical experienced truth that will lead to empowerment, not through socio-political means, but empowerment through intellectual liberation, then the proper method to use is to study the system and be critical of it. Studying the system means knowing it, using it and understanding it. Criticism implies the ability to know that the system exists physically, consciously and as an idea in an individual's mind. To make this leap from the physical to the idea, the individual must step out of the system and observe it objectively from an external perspective. This privilege is only accorded to those who are able to critically think and question. The questions asked cannot be questions that deal with how others feel, but questions that deal with how an individual feels as she is involved within the system.

Eric Hoffer (1951) states that we are afraid of freedom, afraid of not belonging, of having to be responsible for our own actions and not feeling part of a greater whole. We fight to be free from traditional society, yet this freedom leads us to feel isolated. What is freedom then? Individuals in their quest for freedom forget to ask what freedom is. Hoffer believed that they "who clamor loudest for freedom are often the ones least likely to be happy in a free society" (Hoffer, 1951, p. 33). Echoing Hoffer, Erich Fromm (1941), stated that although freedom made us realize our individual self, allowing us to break away from the "pre-individualistic" society, it has also isolated and made us powerless. Karl Popper (1984/1992) provides two interpretations of freedom, one pessimistic (limitation of freedom) and one optimistic (extension of freedom). He states that competition results in the limitation of freedom, at the same time it allows men to search for new possibilities, resulting in an extension of freedom.

When the curriculum-maker is dealing with curriculum today, she must ask how her work will limit or extend freedom. How can truth be a liberating movement for the oppressed masses? Our inspiration for the curricular approach to space is John Dewey (1910). First step in the curriculum process is identifying the problem. The problem is to evolve a curriculum that deals with the conflict of the theoretical (US perception of equality and freedom) and the practical (racial stratification). The second step is to define the problem. How do we capture the learner to come to grips with her own freedom and experiences, while dealing with the ideas of American freedom and realities of racism? The third step is to develop a curriculum, which attacks the problem head-on, allows the individual to step back and become critical, then rejoins society and makes a difference. George Counts believed that the key to social change was schools, and that teachers were going to instill the learners with the ability to make changes (Counts, 1932). The goal is not only to make the individual come to grips with the duality of existence. If each individual can learn to be critical and deal with the conflict, then we can move toward change.

The most difficult step was selecting a solution that would allow for change in individuals. It is our contention that there is a direct and significant relationship between national ideologies and the curriculum. The American mind was unique because of the nation's frontier mentality, open spaces and because no group in an immigrant society is allowed to organize itself coercively, to seize control of public space, or to monopolize public resources (Glazer 1997, p. 32). The uniqueness of the United States was that it was a nation of immigrants, which in no way negates the existence of a dominant cultural identity. However, American culture and mind were willing to accept foreign and different food ways and folkways, incorporating them into the social fabric, while advancing the concept of the American race (Hackett Fischer 1989; Sowell 1981). Henry S. Commager states that the sense of spaciousness, the invitation to mobility, the atmosphere of independence, encouragement to enterprise and to optimism created the American character (Commager 1950, pp. 4–5). Frederick J. Turner also saw America as unique because it took form as its citizens pushed the frontier westward (1899). As the nation expanded westward, there was little concern for internal social issues. As long as there was land to conquer, social problems were not as important. In other words, the American dream was a real and achievable concept. When the land became scarce and expensive, the American Dream was sustained as an ideological commitment to the promise of democracy. George S. Counts (1932) offered the following observation:

> America has been synonymous throughout the world with democracy and symbolic to the oppressed classes of all lands of hope and opportunity. Child of the revolutionary ideas and impulses of the eighteenth century, the American nation became the embodiment of bold social experimentation and a champion of the power of environment to develop the capacities and redeem the souls of common men and women (p. 39).

The forging of the nation was a dynamic and organic process that combines an experimental form of government, an ever changing society, immigrant citizens and a unique concept of law (Wiggin, 1962). An important paradigm to address is the autobiographical paradigm. The autobiographical paradigm allows the person to realize her importance and forces her to return to society in order to make a difference. Counts believed that at the base of American education "there is a profound faith in the potentialities of the individual man" (Counts, 1971, p. 12).

The unifying force that will carry this massive curriculum effort out is democracy. This is a logical journey for free-thinking individuals, who when enlightened will be empowered and set themselves and their society free. This curriculum will not produce what Eric Hoffer (1951) describes as perfect followers who give away their freedom:

The absolute unity and the readiness for self-sacrifice which give an active movement its irresistible drive and enable it to undertake the impossible are usually achieved at a sacrifice of much that is pleasant and precious in the autonomous individual (p. 152).

We hope to establish a twofold purpose to identity, namely metaidentity— experienced through school curriculum. The first purpose for curriculum should be for improvement. The second purpose should be to shift the focus from the entire curriculum to the progress of the individual. Clifford Geertz's notion of "thick description" (Geertz 1973, 1974) contributes to this process in a call for a cooperation of studies between the social sciences and the humanities (1974, pp. ix–xi). Geertz tries to connect the world of the artist (humanities) with the world of the art critic (social sciences). We cannot study place with studying its social implications—racial identity (2005a; 2005b). At the same time, we cannot study racial identity without studying its place. The two are interconnected. Their separation would detract an important aspect of the society, thereby giving an incomplete picture. The same occurs in identity.

We intentionally interfered with the standards visions of time, to rethink the linearity of time and text to allow for the reinterpretation of what counts as place and identity. What concerns us is that educators and reformers need to bracket any notion of specialness in both as empirically insupportable. However defined, place and identity have in general become fundamentally indefinable, and the specialness of each experience is couched more in perceptions than reality.

A person does not individually construct identity, that is to say whiteness, but a case study of some socially constructed peoples can impact how we study place. The "place" of an American is, at once, both place bound and cosmopolitan, resulting ultimately in an economic and geographical reality that is defined by the dominant society. In the U.S., identity became defined because of the economic strife existed as part of a developing industrial and colonial society where individual differences had to become domesticated under the marketplace (Menand, 2000). Thus, group change and identity are not possible because the group has been acculturated in the nature of industrialism and the cult of efficiency. In other words, because of the marketplace, place and identity are intimately dependent on national identity.

For a new curriculum to emerge, we first want to deconstruct and reinterpret the narrow historical narrative to explore boundaries beyond conflicts of place and racial identity. One assertion is in recognizing the definition to encompass the questions of "whom" and not just, what is. In *The Burden of Southern History*,

C. Vann Woodward (1993) warns us that "in a time when nationalism sweeps everything else before it, as it does at present…. America is the all-important subject, and national ideas, national institutions, and national policies are the themes that compel attention." Whiteness has become important to place because it introduces us to the concept of imagined communities, which allows us to focus on the idea of place among rural Americans. Concurrently, there is room for creating space. C. Vann Woodward states that, "every self-conscious group of any size fabricates myths about its past: about its origins, its mission, its righteousness, its benevolence, its general superiority" (Woodward, 1993, p. 12). After raising this issue, he then argues that although groups believe themselves to be unique, they were not (Woodward, 1993). Real or not, this ideology provoked real effects. George Tindall believed that myths like those surrounding place, had a tendency to lay "the ground for belief, for either loyalty and defense on the one hand or hostility and opposition on the other" (Tindall, 1964, p. 2). This connection is the strongest bond within the imagined community and hardest to break, especially when dealing with race. The individual makes a connection to their past through values and rituals which are natural outgrowths of the surrounding situations.

If place is a result of oppression, how do the oppressed gain identity that belongs to them? Edmund Morgan suggests that the relationship between the oppressor (industrialism) and the oppressed (blacks) was a negotiated relationship between human beings. He states that "it is much easier to view them as tyrants and victims, and to displaced contempt by a condescending feeling of guilt that secretly blames the victim" (Morgan, 1975, p. 16). Victims inspire guilt but seldom respect. Respect comes from actions undertaken by the oppressed. Places chose to leave the collective agrarian society and integrate into the dominant industrial culture. The vehicle was not of their making, but the action to choose was of their own accord (Onuf, 1989).

Important to our argument is that while the organization of schools and their cultures of teaching are virtually identical, or at least fundamentally uniform, we do not believe that this requires a uniform or standardized response. Precisely because of the diversity of communities, we hold that standardization is not an appropriate response. The sheer diversity of place would suggest to us that the solution must be local not general. The context of community, local and regional culture, family lives and so on, would direct us to nonstandardized schools; to emulate the standardization movement is wrongheaded precisely because it is designed to ignore local contexts. Place-based education and the like are thus a partial solution.

Researchers can distinguish themselves by confronting and admitting the general problem schools share and to not get defensive when critics like us say schooling is pretty much the same everywhere in the U.S. and there is nothing really special about each school. They too face the problem of improving curriculum and instruction and moving away from the calcified cultures of teaching and extraordinarily limited notions of knowledge they inhere. Hanging on to practices that are intellectually limiting, however "effective" they have been in the past, or engaging in some futile attempt to emulate the decontextualized accountability schemes that are pressed by the standards movement, may hasten their own demise and lead other critics to say, "See, they can't keep up or make themselves better."

Researchers can help this situation by setting aside conventional notions of "place" and identity as defined by location and by abandoning assumption of specialness of practices, i.e., in effect, there is no such thing as "place" and identity as a generalized or generalizable phenomena. By construing place as a symbolic maps and identity and schools as part of an imagined community, researchers are on firmer ground to consider education in its varied contexts—both the "objective" form in location and the "subjective" form in the minds of all people. Moreover, this permits the researcher to squarely face the general problem of instruction created by a generalized school system and culture of teaching while considering a local response in such things as "place-based" education and identity.

Designing Curriculum

In his profound text, *The Transformation of the School*, Lawrence Cremin (1961) connects science, Darwinism and education. He points out the nature of the moment, linking the great minds in psychology, social theory and philosophy that together shaped a movement which would become the foundation upon which education in America would be based. From a populist perspective, Darwin's theory of survival of the fittest was easy to understand and embraced by individuals such as William Graham Sumner who espoused his beliefs about society: If we do not like the survival of the fittest we have only one possible alternative, and that is the survival of the unfittest. The former is the law of civilization; the latter is the law of anti-civilization (Commager, 1950, p. 202). The arguments of the day focused on society's obligations to the masses resulting in a social paradox descriptive of the

American experience. Whereas Sumner advocated laissez-faire, Lester Frank Ward argued that it was incoherent, fragmentary, insincere, and futile, scarcely consistent with the law of nature and wholly inconsistent with the law of man (Commager, 1950, p. 207) there was to be no resolution to this argument. Over time the spiral moved toward social efficiency but the path required passing though the influence of Northern Industrialism. As stated earlier, social efficiency was an obvious answer to the question of integrating different cultures into a single society through education. The need to acculturate the immigrants was a logistical concern as the schools where charged with the task of social assimilation—the building of the American race. For Kliebard (1995/2004), Progressivism was an intellectual bazaar, as neither in terms of the coherence of the program for reform, nor in its membership, nor in its overall ideology can a definition of progressivism as a social and political movement be articulated (Kliebard, 1995/2004, p. 240). However, it is important to recall that progressives were conservative in nature and aligned with contemporary thought (Karier 1975, p. xxi). Franklin Bobbitt (1918) provided a systematic framework for the scientific evaluation of educational programs, to facilitate mass education. Jane Addams advocated the study of children and their social environment as the basis for determining the path for program development (Addams, 1905). For Charles Prosser the influence of science affected all social institutions (Prosser, 1916). George E. Vincent (1990) believed that since education was a socializing process, sociology had to be applied to the study of both children and schooling. Finally, John Dewey (1910) stated:

> ... even where science has achieved its most attentive recognition, it has remained a servant of ends imposed from alien traditions. If ever we are to be governed by intelligence, not by things and words, science must have something to say about what we do, and not merely about how we do it most easily and economically (p. 127).

Habermas (1992) stated that the individual must be rescued from complete absorption into the particular contexts in which she is always embedded. If our objective is to have each individual attain critical self-examination, then our model should be built around the three paradigms. The paradigms will have a connection to each child's personal experiences. This aspect will be explored in the next section of the chapter. The key lies in each individual's self-awareness. The problem is that "the opposition to change and innovation in schools is pervasive, and many curriculum leaders abandon their efforts to reconceptualize teaching and learning for lack of support"

(Slattery, 1995, p. 10). For Slattery (1995), "postmodernism challenges educators to explore a worldview that envisions schooling through a difference lens of indeterminacy, aesthetics, autobiography, intuition, eclecticism and mystery" (p. 23). In *Dare the School Build a New Social Order?*, Counts (1932) required that teachers be the leaders of the revolution that changed and improved democracy.

Elliot Eisner (1979/2006) emphasizes that time is crucial to change. Sometimes programs are not given a chance to prove themselves. Ideas have to be given a chance to cause change. "They are historical and transitory products" (Shapiro in Cranston & Mair, 1980, p. 159). Ideas are dynamic, some catch on quickly and cause immediate change, others take time and cause change over time. For example, many of the civil rights reformers had been educated after World War II, when they were taught that the war was fought to end the racist and fascist regime of Germany. The lessons they learned in school took almost twenty years to manifest themselves.

As Margaret Latta (2001) emphasizes, curriculum evaluation is a process of searching that has to constantly be kept in mind. Latta also asks the participants to be active in the process, as teachers, learners and researchers to build a collaborative culture of educational research, from which flexible and high-functioning research can become a magnet for the participants to advance their own knowledge of and expertise in curriculum; contribute to the education of new teachers by helping them understand the importance of educational practice, the impact it has on their work, and their own role within education; and involve classroom teachers and educational leaders in the investigation of teaching and learning by undertaking research so that they are not merely subjects of and sites for research, but active contributors to the development of knowledge. If Latta's words are heeded, then the evaluating process will be fostered as a constant and critical shadow of the curricular process.

Anger forces the individual to reexamine themselves. It is not necessarily a good or bad approach. It, like any other feeling is a subset of its context. When norms and values are questioned and begin to show their inconsistences, individuals must decide what their identity has defined them as. Individuals try to achieve a comfort balance that keeps us from having to face the conflict between what we know and do not know, as the constraints of knowledge restraint us. Another misinterpretation of teenagers, especially in popular culture, is a derogatory view of their cognitive sophistication to interpret and re/interpret their identity, more so than adults.

The autobiographical nature of this project is what postmodernist curriculum makers are asking for in our schools because it "challenge[s] educators to begin with the individual experience and then make broader connections (Slattery, 1995, p. 58). The autobiographical connection to the broader society cannot be made in schools without addressing the structured and closed Tylerian model (Tyler, 1949) of school curriculum. Dewey always believed that the school would allow the child self-recognition and a link to society. How to connect the freedom of learning with a society obsessed with quantization. This alienation of the individual from the structure is what reformers have in the past addressed through autobiography. Pinar, in Slattery (1995) states that "we can no longer remain ahistorical, detached, impersonal, and 'behaviorally objective" (p. 66). Thus, without an understanding of the linear model of schools and a language from which to challenge and change this model, individuals cannot change their position while ignoring the linear nature of institutions. Poststructuralists have suggested that the individual become aware, and act without structural functional society (Smart, 1993). In an ironic twist, that approach broadens the curricular schism by ultimately alienating the individual from the curriculum. In the end, the change might or might not occur, however, that is up to the individual. In a sense the individual falls into Marx's dichotomy of existence, wanting to be free from the structure but giving up the path to that agency that lies within the structure. This schism has surfaced many times in debates within the field, yet the field itself has never made an attempt to address it publicly leading to a peripheral role in educational reform. In *Good Will Hunting*, a psychologist tries to channel Will Hunting's intelligence in a "positive" way. In a climactic scene, a professor argues with his best friend, the psychiatrist, that a person who has knowledge and does not share it with society is not being fair to the rest of us. It is more important to share your knowledge, no matter how small, than it is to keep it to oneself. In Cuba, Dr. Carlos Finlay discovered a cure for Yellow Fever. Cubans were immune, but Americans were not. If cured, Americans would stay in Cuba. Yet, he still shared his knowledge with the American occupying forces. Our duty to society far outweighs our individual needs.

Barry Smart (1993) states that poststructuralism is the "humanization of technology" (p. 2). How does the learner humanize technology? The humanization of technology is quite easy. For example, computers and software have become our masters. We accuse them of sabotage, we ask of them for help, and we rely on them for information on what to do—all as if they were people. Instead, we should use them to construct knowledge, build connections, and ultimately change the world. It becomes a class issue of whether the instrument is a new tool of the bourgeoisie or the technological representation of the bourgeoisie itself.

How does that solve our problem of the conflict between the theories of freedom and the practice of racial stratification? Humanizing a mechanical society leads to a new awareness of people that we shape society. This connection must be channeled so that the individual can truly have the tools (language) to shape society. It is worthless to be free and critical of oneself and of society without taking the next step: changing society. Spirituality is essential here. Slattery (1995) states that a "constructive poststructural vision of schooling in the contemporary global community includes an eclectic and ecumenical integration of spirituality and theology into the very fabric of education" (p. 68). Habermas (1992) states that:

> Extra mundane perspective of a "God's-eye view" a perspective radically different from the lines of sight belonging to inner worldly participants and observers. Negative metaphysics uses the perspective of the radical outsider, mad, isolated, or aesthetically enraptured, he who distances himself from the life world as a whole. To no longer have a language, no speech based on based on reasons, for spreading the message of that which they have seen. Speechlessness finds words only in the empty negation of everything that metaphysics once affirmed with the concept of the universal One (p. 51).

In spirituality there is a duality between the freedom that the individuality of the connection between the I and the Other offers as well as a unifying community feeling the individual feels in unification with others who are of like thought. This dual existence is not conflictive, but joyous. This relation can be used to infuse the removed individual into the dehumanized society in order to cause social change. Why do we join religious groups? We need spirituality in our lives. Although we might not agree with the practice of the institution (church) we still continue to deal with the Other. Isolationism is social death. That is why we hold on to archaic social structures.

How does the individual deal with the love of the Other and the hate of her religion toward those that are different? The liberated individual forces change. How? Although we pretend not to be spiritual, our lives have a goal, earthly or otherworldly. Anger causes change. Anger causes us to change our goal or work harder to achieve them. Hoffer (1951) believed that dissatisfaction causes change and that comfort leads to satisfaction. We thrive in comfort, ignoring conflict. If conflict is brought out we have to solve it. A "free" individual has taken the step from World One (physical) to World Three (critical). The search for truth is constant and never-ending. Looking for falsity in reality is how we prove that we are heading for the truth (Popper, 1984/1992, p. 38). We are preoccupied with problem solving, finding our place in the world through active participation (13).

Autobiographical Paradigm of Place

This paradigm allows the individual to form dyadic and other personal relationships within a dehumanizing paradigm. Small groups, unlike individuals, can cause significant change. For example, if one plantation mistress can teach a slave boy to read (Frederick Douglass) causing change in his life, imagine if a group of mistresses taught many boys to read, what would the change be? Even if the action served to satisfy her own guilt and not to help Douglass, this action can lead to immense societal change: revolution. Slattery states that "poststructural curriculum challenges students to enter history rather than simply observe history from a distance" (Slattery, 1995, 38). In poststructuralism, the learners must act as "participants rather than as observers" (Slattery, 1995, 39). Poststructuralists' problems rest not with the curriculum, but like Ivan Illich (1971), their conflict is with the institutionalization of learning.

For Popper "criticism consists in the search for contradiction and in their elimination: the difficulty created by the demand for their elimination constitutes a new problem" (Popper 1972, 126). The first step in social change is applying this set of questions to the new liberated student. Popper (1984/1992) states that solutions are open to criticism and we must attempt to refute them, if the solution fails our criticism, we propose another, if it survives we "accept it worthy of further discussion and criticism" (66). Our new philosophy is "not simply a study of perennial truths but rather a vehicle for engendering justice, compassion, self-exploration, empowerment, critical thinking, and, ... ecological sustainability in a threatened global environment" (Slattery, 1995, 168). Popper (1984/1992) believes that humans think in three worlds, (1) physical, (2) conscious, and (3) critical. Curriculum should strive to function in the third world.

The U.S. is a race conscious nation and society; race drives our ideas because of our past. Yet, our language does not deal with this problem. According to Popper, the "shaping of reality is the interaction between the solid [World 1], conscious [World 2] and objective [World 3]. We the human mind, our dreams, our objectives–are the creator of the work, of the product, and at the same time we are shaped by our work" (Popper, 1984/1992, p. 26). At the same time we create, we can transform ourselves through our work. In dealing with our theory and praxis through language, we will feel uncomfortable. Critical truth is not easy, yet without it we can never end our conflict.

· 5 ·

URBAN SPACES

Introduction

What we hope to convey in this chapter is that muddy conceptual foundations prevent eclecticism in research and the framing of problems for thinking about the stewardship of higher education that should be driving research and outreach (Bennett et al., 2012). In response to this problem we propose a conceptual framework of stewardship in higher education for educational research that moves beyond location and focuses on the historical-spatial identity of the institution (Callejo et al., 2004). We propose a conceptual approach to place, to recreate a sense of hope of what urban communities and reforms will look like for communities and their stakeholders, while allowing the change to both remain grounded in its mission and adjust to the changing nature of the economy and politics.

Essential to the spirit of this work is how communities can move beyond the rhetoric of stewardship to actual practice through the changing of what counts as innovation, schooling, and place. We need to envision, create, and sustain multiple organizational spaces in which institutions recognize their relationships with their communities and explore possibilities within and among themselves. We must develop a comprehensive system of professional support, through the development of operational spaces to help communities focus on the more human nature of their work and thus positively impact change that promotes innovation, within a culture of transparency that promotes effective operation and governance that supports community development. Within this space all stakeholders have the most to contribute, and as such, should be the most engaged internally and externally.

Sadly, change in urban communities always leans toward the failure of the poor, people of color, and diverse language learners. There is little or no proactive action that seeks to offer alternative points of view as to what constitutes public spaces of power and whether stakeholders are actually becoming free within those movements (Dittmer, 1995; Katz 1968).

I suggest that community leaders look inward and reassess how they measure change. We have to keep in mind, that the impetus, planning, and support for the community-centered change and empowerment come from outside the state and local school districts. The reformers, who are ultimately legally responsible to their benefactors (funders, foundations, politicians), the federal government, do not take into account the unique contexts of communities. Ironically, few of us have devoted serious time to what communities we work in or live are about, or what ideals they should be trying to achieve; instead, we often cling to the notion of local control while allowing external and impersonal sojourners to make the most important decisions about and for communities. The major problem with urban policy today is that too much decision-making takes place in Washington and within corporations instead of in communities and homes of those impacted. These conversations and their consequences often take us by surprise; because we often never see changes coming. Some of us choose merely to accommodate and follow mandates, no matter how obtuse or ill-informed they may be. Others choose to call themselves "change agents" and state that their purpose is to drive knowledge when in reality they limit its growth. What follows is the narrative of one community in Michigan, which we are calling the Federal District, which has attempted to remake itself from within by remaining true to its identity.

Place and History of the Federal District

Located in the shadow of Interstate 94 in Southern Michigan near Detroit, the Federal District is starting to catch its breath. Once a vibrant neighborhood of prosperity, where 19th century executives built their grand mansions and blue-collar families lived in middle class homes, the Federal District was a main link in the once strong industrial supply chain for more than a century. At the turn of the 21st century, the neighborhoods bound together within the District were overwhelmed by a manufacturing consolidation that took hold well before the financial crisis. What remained was a common rust-belt story: concentrated poverty, lack of trust in authorities and services, and desperate crime amid pockets of once-majestic homes. Those that could leave for better opportunity did long ago. When relief did not come, the District re-made itself. Weekly meetings were well attended and an identity was reborn from its history and visions for a new future. Where identity was once enveloped by shame and poverty, today a District watches its volunteers scan empty lots for crime, cleaning its streets, and seeking economic partnerships for a newly revitalized main thoroughfare. When the momentum caught the attention of the political leadership, a home ownership program was developed, and a youth center extended the education day and created anti-gang organizing efforts. St. John's Hospital and the businesses of Jefferson Avenue, anchoring the southern corner of the District, began investing their own capital into cleaning up the lawns, streets, and sidewalks. While the economic revitalization is alive, and the momentum is palpable, the Federal District neighborhood is realizing progress, although their revitalization plan is slow and many times fraught with setbacks. Although hazardous structures are torn down, streetlights functioning, and grass cut; District redevelopment, in the eyes of neighbors and leaders, remains unfulfilled. While the physical assets are being repaired, attention must be given to the human capital and the social services to achieve the hope of the citizens. We must humanize those involved in creating curricular spaces as they develop their neighborhoods.

Indicators of Need in a Spatial Context

As the 21st century began, many of the most vexing problems confronting humanity in the 20th century were not resolved. Education has to be among the highest priority human needs for a number of reasons, including the empowerment of people to change their life situations, the enhancement of national economic growth, and the promotion of sustainable development. While governments and private organizations have responded in many ways, continued growth in the number of children, especially in rural areas, make it difficult to respond to these educational needs. In addition, the skills and knowledge that are required from or used by the working age population have changed rapidly in the last decades. The need for continued education or adult education adds another task to the crowded agenda facing educational planners in formal and informal educational programs that contribute to both societal and individual development of communities that address historically low performing public schools, racial disparity, and high infant mortality.

Vision for the Public Spaces: Even with reasons for despair, Federal District residents look to the years ahead, envisioning school buildings functioning as a hub—becoming full service communities. Incentives could be used to fill morning and evening programs for parents and children, promoting a culture of well-being in the community. A health clinic embedded in the schools could address a menu of student and family needs. Community gardens would address the food desert and provide needed healthy food options. The school building could move into full community center each evening. Students and community members could be able to access the library, computer labs, and gym. Recreational classes, dance, art, and marching band could be offered at the building. Field trips could be arranged for Friday afternoons and evenings to help students understand their neighborhood, and places beyond its boundaries. Community service projects could be planned and implemented by students monthly, empowering a sense of ownership. On the weekends, community sports teams could use the gym. On Saturday mornings, special topic lectures could offer interactive learning experiences to engage children, adults, and even seniors, in a variety of educational opportunities. In sum, the Federal District could become a community where education has no age requirement and where the school activities are integrated into everyday life making a neighborhood. Throughout this process, running parallel to the neighborhood's efforts, the city is alleviating the blight and revitalizing the business community. Where low-cost, but nutritionally void food options once stood, a new grocery could open and offer fresh produce and healthy food. Residents could congregate at the local credit union, and folks could catch coffee at the corner restaurant on their way to work.

Collaborating to Build Public Spaces: In order to create change, stakeholders have to serve as leaders and catalysts in removing the institutional barriers between efforts across the communities. To attain this ambitious vision, communities have to build cohesion across all stakeholders, including local government, business, community organizations, service providers, schools, and most importantly—all its members. Only then can we begin to understand and build empathy toward all persons, regardless of the social space they occupy.

Stakeholders and Curricular Spaces for Action

Central themes drive change and creation of curricular spaces. We argue that in urban areas impact needs to be viewed through measurable problems such as: (1) infant mortality, which is an indicator to many factors impacting success in schools and is also directly a result of race inequality, where the goal is to decrease the African American infant mortality (19.1 from 2007–2009) to the national average (5.7 per 1,000 live births) and (2) disconnected youth, which is related to a large number of 16–24 year olds who are living outside the social and economic infrastructure of the community. In the Federal District more than 3,800 out-of-school youth (14% of total youth ages 16–24) are disconnected from education and the labor market. Lacking workplace skills or opportunities, these youth face dismal future of long-term unemployment, poverty, substance abuse, and/or incarceration. Addressing these measureable goals allows stakeholders to have attainable measures that will bear impact.

Leveraging Existing Neighborhood Assets

Collaboration is paramount to this initiative's success. The Federal District stakeholders spent a significant part building relationships and promoting collaboration among service providers in the District along with community members. This effort aimed to coordinate current services to ensure redundancies do not exist among service providers in the District. Additionally, stakeholders sought out opportunities to learn from similar efforts in Michigan, the Midwest, and the nation at large. This was decided because of limited resources, that the stakeholders would learn from other communities' work.

Researching Solutions with a Heart: The Role of Education

Two overarching principles should provide the framework for this work. First, education should be holistic rather than merely school-based, and second, integrated services tend to be more efficient and likely to be maintained. We must also recognize that "more" is not always "better" and that fragmented, piecemeal programs are less likely to be effective and maintained (Adelman & Taylor, 2006). Along this line, coordination of programming efforts with local, state, and national initiatives and priority is important. Schools must shift their focus to community-based leadership, where they shift partnership emphasis to schools and the Federal District. The key component is the founding of advisory subgroups (education, health, and economics) with representation from community, providers, and evaluators who analyze data and make recommendation, based on community needs, history, and practices.

The model employed is an approach where those who deliver services learn from the constituents and become not just service providers but students of the community. In exchange, the community members learn as well as educate service providers about their community. Schools and community organizations must embrace the idea of evaluation; they need to be seen as "communities" and begin to adopt principles of responsive evaluation that improves communities, schools and learners, while addressing the relationship between research and communities' needs that serves to harness local resources into collaborative projects that become models for community growth. The key is in identifying local individuals to serve in many of the required roles. The community was able to leverage its frequent work with a number of talented individuals with the specialized knowledge necessary to achieve the objectives—they are confident this team will represent a blend of local knowledge and specialized experience necessary to complete the work. Several ideas emerged for the importance of sustainability, such as diverse perspectives, local capacity, and research and evaluation.

Incorporating Diverse Perspectives. Previous neighborhood revitalization efforts in the Federal District created advisory boards comprised of residents to help in their planning and implementation efforts. These groups became active community organizations and provided essential insight into the community throughout this process and also lend legitimacy to the effort among residents, essential for this initiative's success.

Building Local Capacity. The long-term success of the District depends on informed decision-making and collaboration between services provided and shared data. As such, two essential objectives were: (1) creating an integrated data system that ensures easy and comprehendible *access* to data and (2) building capacity to *utilize* data in decision-making around three important issues (infant mortality, obesity, and disconnected youth). This will result in increasing families' abilities to have primary decision-making roles in their children's care, provide access to quality education and health pro-grams within the district for children and parents and culturally responsive health and educational services for parents, children, and youth. The goal was to successfully and permanently reengage more disconnected youth with educational opportunities and work experiences and build collaboration across disconnected youth-serving agencies and systems in the county to pro-vide effective shared, network-wide outcome measures, client service process, and data management.

Building on momentum of previous efforts, the District expand the data's utility. Data must be able to quantitatively and qualitatively assess our community's needs, and subsequently guide the design and implementation of programs. Moving data from a compliance function to a research function will be especially pertinent during our planning year. Clear data must be shared across systems, empowering decision-makers at all levels, from the mayor or doctor to a mother or teacher. Data should inform stakeholders about the performance of youth, both in the aggregate and down to the individual. Data should be available to investors. Reliable, valid, readily available data allow us to provide program evaluations and additional insights into outcomes for current and potential supporters. Finally, as program success should be evalu-ated using measurable objectives. A longitudinal data system, combined with training in utilizing data, will facilitate the quantitative and qualitative assess-ment of both short and long term outcomes.

The assessment process included interviews with partners to assess informa-tion needs for reporting on indicators, focus group interviews with families and students to bring their voices into the planning process, development of longi-tudinal files for analytic studies supporting partners, and collaboration with the partners to provide information and technical support for assessment and action inquiry. Consistent with the goals for system development interview of leaders and system administrators involved in supporting systems for public schools, health systems, and community organizations that supported the District were conducted. A strategy for integration of reporting on indicators and data-rich decision-making was created and focus interviews were conducted with par-ents in schools and community centers and students. Interviews were ana-lyzed to assess perceptions of financial barriers to college and career pathways, social support needs and trust of support networks, and cultural capital (college knowledge and support for educational and financial uplift). This qualitative assessment method provided valuable information for program design and will be used in assessment reports informing SNP partners and community groups.

A baseline assessment of poverty levels, employment and educational attainment for the District using Census data on block groups and longitudinal data on students provided the base against which future progress would be measured. Current and developed data systems were used to generate data for analytic studies of programs and long-term evaluation of interventions.

To ensure the data system is most useful to the District and the region, an information system that was (1) comprehensive; (2) longitudinal; (3) accessible to a variety of users, and (4) available in real time (providing rapid-time data) was developed.

Comprehensive data across the County were collected and stored by a variety of agencies and shared only in exceptional circumstances. The stakeholders recognized the need to collaborate in programming. Program officers across the continuum of services needed to have access to a data system that allows a complete picture of students and the community at large.

Longitudinal data allowed assessment of progress against long-term outcomes. Stakeholders needed the support of a longitudinal data system to track students through educational transitions by adding prenatal to pre-Kindergarten and postsecondary data to the K-12 system. This tracking system provided the core data for tracking cohorts of students through critical transitions: from early childhood to kindergarten (with links to health and community service); from K to 4th grade (with links to family involvement in reading programs); from 5th to 8th grade (to track development of basic skills and family engagement); from 9th to 12th grade (to track engagement, achievement, and transition to high school); and from high school into college enrollment (to track academic preparation and enrollment). The cohort files for these transitions were organized and analyzed to identify barriers to each transition (to inform planning and implementation) and practices associated with successful transitions. Feasibility of alternative information collection strategies will be examined as part of the assessment process. For example, a web-based, open access survey and counseling system—could be used to assess student interests and track both student and parent involvement in services.

Accessibility to many users was important to maximize accessibility; updates on achievement of indicators and results of research analyses were made available to District partners. The reporting on indicators will draw from a number of existing data sources and present information in a common access point. The data system design process came from assessment of partners' information and research needs—this became an integral data source for design of reporting processes and analytic studies.

Analytic and Evaluation Studies provided analyses of longitudinal data on student cohorts broken down by Census block groups as a means of establishing the baseline for poverty, work patterns, and educational attainment against which future progress can be measured. Census blocks were used to track students in groups. The longitudinal cohort data, broken down by Census block groups, evaluated current and new practices on an ongoing basis after the initial assessment. Targeted evaluation studies to identify successful practices that could be improved, if necessary, and brought to scale were examined. Analytic studies using student cohort data provided tools for evaluations of current and past practices. The long-term evaluation strategy focused on interventions pilot tested and brought to scale by action teams. SNP practitioners (teachers, community organizers, health care workers, etc.) will be studied using cohort databases, surveys and interview.

Institutional Cohesion and Identity: How Schools can Lead Change

Research, Albers (1965) writes, is the ability to search and search again—to see as Hannah Arendt (Passerin d'Entrèves, 1993) suggests, the idea of fragmentary historiography, one that seeks to identify the moments of rupture, displacement, and dislocation in history. Such fragmentary historiography enables one to recover lost potentials of the past, in the hope that they may find actualization in the present. For Arendt (1958), "It is necessary to redeem from those past moments worth preserving, to save fragments from past treasures that are significant for us" (p. 4). Only against the grain of traditionalism and the claims of conventional historiography can the past be made meaningful again, provide sources of illumination for the present, and yield its treasures to those who search for them with "new thoughts" and saving acts of remembrance (Passerin d'Entrèves, p. 5). Robert Dahl (1970) wrote "though you would find it less tidy, it would not be absurd for you to start with your own proposed solutions and work backward" (p. 166). In order for us to become active in school leadership educators need to move away from the current disinvestment occurring in our public schools and develop proposals for change in our schools (Molnar, 1986).

In response, educators need to develop tools that make thinking visible. Specifically, schools need to gather their own evidence of thinking. School leaders have unique insights on their learners' creative thinking, problem solving, and most importantly, the connections they make to themselves, others, texts, and the world. School leaders need to invite parents as co-observers. Historically, schools and teachers have had adversarial relationships with our parents, mainly over the moral and religious content. Schools should invite parents to invest in the common cause that is the education of their children. Last, school leaders need to think about data as a living and dynamic history of their schools. As Dahl (1970) writes, revolutions emerge from individual solutions to common problems. We need to consider all solutions—search out multiple successful ways to measure thinking.

Transformative leadership occurs when leaders are attuned with those they lead and remain empathic throughout the process without becoming oppressive themselves. Burns' thought process is similar to that of Freire (1970/1997) and Arendt (1958), who valued empathy and power in relations among the oppressed, oppressors, and liberators. Arendt (1958) explained that those deprived of seeing and hearing others and of being seen and heard by others "are all imprisoned in the subjectivity of their own singular experience, which does not cease to be singular if the same experience is multiplied innumerable times ... seen only under one aspect and is permitted to present itself in only one perspective" (p. 58). In the foreword to the 1997 edition of *Pedagogy of the Oppressed*, Richard Shaull states that Freire:

> Operates on one basic assumption: that man's ontological vocation (as he [Freire] calls it) is to be a Subject who acts upon and transforms his world and in so doing moves toward ever new possibilities of fuller and richer life individually and collectively (p. 14).

Freire (1970) declares, "pedagogy of the oppressed must be animated by authentic, humanistic (not humanitarian) generosity and present itself as pedagogy of human kind (p. 36)." Concurrently, transactional leadership functions on a system that exchanges performance for rewards or punishment; however, the exchange could be social, political, philosophical, economic, or psychological. The relationship among people remains as long as the common interest is maintained—goods such as votes or money are bargained though participants have no investment other than an understanding that they need each other. Once the arrangement is over, participants may choose to go on their separate ways. In education, this relationship is mistakenly seen as transformative—although not unique to education as seen by the current debate on health care where disparate groups are attempting to exchange goods for votes—we use transformative language to describe these simple acts of transactional leadership. Burns (1978/1982) clearly uses transformative leadership and transactional leadership to differentiate between management as method and leadership as art. What is ironic is that we continue to use transformative leadership to describe and justify any action we label reform.

Curriculum as transformative leadership

Curriculum design and evaluation provide a set of standards based on short term goals that seek to respond to pre-determined skill- and content-based subject learning. The dominance of such curriculum pervasive in schools is based narrowly on ideas of change and reform—seeking to align performance on math and reading (achievement gap) to the larger social issues of poverty and race. With apologies to Charles Dickens, it is the best of times; it is the worst of times. It is an age of unprecedented spending for program growth; it is an age of record budget deficits and cutbacks. In countless school districts across America, new programs have risen to replace traditional ones and accommodate a growing number of students. Yet, a faltering economy has put the squeeze on operating budgets and has made constituents less likely to support ambitious construction proposals. So, as programs and alternatives open at record pace, new graduates are falling behind because they are taught in programs that are inadequate and unsupported. According to Linda Darling Hammond (1999; 2001) and the National Center for Educational Statistics (NCES), today more than ever inequality is evident across all programs, especially in reform-driven programs that seek to "improve performance" (Constantine, Player, Silva, Hallgren, Grider & Deke, 2009).

Schools are allowed to be representations of a slice of life, conceptualized as an organized totality, in which elements are not separable, and therefore, cannot be separately studied. In this environment, education is constantly occurring and evolving. Schooling must strike a balance between methodology and curriculum (accountability) and interpretation and curriculum (curiosity). Dewey (1934) describes what transformational leadership and transformational leaders could be when he states that:

> I do not think that the dancing and singing of even little children can be explained wholly on the basis of unlearned and unformed responses to then existing objective occasions. Clearly there must be something in the present to evoke happiness. But the act is expressive only far as it represents unison of something stored from past experience, something therefore generalized, with present conditions (p. 71).

Schools and communities, like the children described by Dewey, have lost their sense of self and play. In focusing on methodology and not interpretation we lose the essence of what schooling is: the search for knowledge. Eisner (1998) is not concerned with methods or approach but with the notion of seeing. His notion of the educational experience encompasses any situation that involves interactions between groups of people where learning leads to changes in one's outlook (1979/2008). Given Eisner's challenge to leadership, I believe we need to examine practice and what can be done to change how transformative leadership is realized.

Concurrently the focus of compulsory education is driven by both professions (law, medicine, engineering, teaching, business, health, etc.) and universities that suggest university training focus on job training that will develop our graduates to be ready to enter the labor force out of college. Is it possible to establish academic foundations for the formation of our graduates with those communities and their anti-intellectual interests (Hofstadter 1963; Slater, Callejo Perez, & Fain, 2008)? Can emphasis on democratic action, such as demand for equal health care for all be a legitimate curricular concern for schools? In *Dare the Schools Build a New Social Order?*, Counts (1932) wrote that schools had the duty to acculturate students to act as democratic citizens and demand social equality and civil rights. When Bobbitt (1918) was hired to create a curriculum for the Los Angeles Public Schools, questions of workers' rights, women's rights, and economic independence were left out of the curriculum. In the home economics curriculum, specific lessons were developed to properly instruct young women how to be better wives (Kliebard, 1995/2004). In re-thinking our curriculum for change, we should ask questions such as, *What practical experiences could our students', experiences bring to their own development?* Dewey (1897; 1910) and Eisner (1979/2008) agree that evaluation of learning is best determined by the individual. Eisner (1979/2008, pp. 203–210) suggests that:

1. tasks used to evaluate what the students know and can do need to reflect the tasks they will encounter in the world outside schools, not those limited to schools themselves. Evaluation tasks should incorporate more than one possible solution and one possible answer to a problem.
2. tasks should have curricular relevance limited by the curriculum itself.
3. tasks should require students to display sensitivity to configurations or wholes, not simply discrete elements.

4. tasks should permit the student to select a form of representation they choose to use to display what has been learned.
5. The tasks used to evaluate students should reveal how students go about solving a problem, not only the solutions they formulated.
6. tasks should reflect the values of the intellectual community from which they are derived.
7. tasks need not be limited to solo performance. Many of the most important tasks we undertake require group efforts.

The predicament in creating change is that society is suffering from an inertia born out of a helpless marriage to economic utility. Schools' reliance on the capitalist sphere has not only tainted the curriculum but also re-oriented students to accept a new kind of reward, "economic utility." So that graduates are told to study not for knowledge sake but to get "well-paying jobs" in the future (Postman 1995, p. 27).

In response to the problem of place-based education and race, we propose a conceptual framework of place-base for analysis of identity that moves beyond location and focuses on historical-spatial identity—specifically meaning making. In this approach to space, to recreate a sense of what educational research and reforms might mean for teaching and learning in communities. The notions that have dominated place-based education and diversity have focused on the ideological of language at the expense of the ontological meanings of place and diversity. We intentionally tamper with standard visions of time, space, text and discourse allowing for the reinterpretation of what counts as place and rural identity using social geographic "mapping" (Soja 1971; 1989). This perspective allows the map reader to imagine an inclusive landscape. This, in turn, permits a definition of community that encompasses and moves beyond negative geographical location and history; envisioning the robust sense of place for research and reform that rural landscapes encompass. The deconstructive approach discussed can give the teacher an understanding of the individual's reality by revealing alternative meanings and thus promote meaning making. The idea of a single truth or meaning is thus challenged (especially in the curriculum). Text can generate a variety of meanings in excess of what is intended—language is not a stable system of correspondences of words to objects, but a sprawling limitless web where there is constant circulation of elements (Eagleton, 1983, p. 129). The meaning of a word depends on its relation to other words, specifically, its difference from other words. The difference is accentuated by an interrelated and hierarchical system of oppositions, i.e. white and black, where each is defined in terms of what the other is not; and where the first member of the pair is considered "more valuable and a guide to truth" (Nehamas, 1987, p. 32).

The problem this leaves for communities and schools—both empirical and linguistic—is that those who are concerned about place and education in particular are constantly constrained to define "placed" as something that it is not. On the one hand, there is an inherent feature of western language systems and, therefore, western thought and, by extension, our own everyday cognition. On the other hand, in the absence of a more established language (*langue*) in both every day and systematic academic use (*parole*)—where we are left to constantly view place as a negative, what it is not.

Community members bring with them a world of experience and knowledge derived from their practice. They have a plurality of experiences derived from what Berger (1974) calls the "pluralisation of lifeworlds." Students have also been educated and in institutions described as oppressive and dehumanizing (Apple, 1986; Illich, 1971; Giroux, 1988; & Katz, 1968). In such systems "motivation has to be analyzed in terms of the characteristics of the basic security system" (Giddens, 1991, p. 64), and curriculum is to be followed and not created. The hope is for students to see the "existential question of self-identity [as] bound in the fragile nature of the biography which the individual 'supplies' about themselves" (54). Providing spaces for the creation of language and its expression through curriculum, students can see and reinvent their biography through the sharing of narratives and shaping of the curriculum. As Giddens (1991) states, "a person's identity is not to be found in behaviour, nor—important though this is—in the reactions of others, but in the capacity *to keep a particular narrative going*" (p. 54).

While educators currently recognize that teaching and learning are complex activities that cannot be divorced from the social and cultural contexts that frame individuals and classrooms, research shows that most educators feel inadequate when it comes to addressing diversity in today's classrooms (US GAO, July 2009). In this book we acknowledge an inadequacy and growing discomfort with diversity taken up in distinct conceptual categories such as race, ethnicity, gender, and culture, stemming from our experiences within the concrete realties of classroom life that tell us diversity is much more complicated in nature. Milligan (2001) writes that the inadequacy of these concepts in the literature where they are often reduced solely to identification and descriptive purposes should create discomfort in us. His confrontation with stereotypical assumptions regarding race, ethnicity, gender, and class, suggests to us the necessity of an ontological understanding of diversity thus assuming reciprocity between self and other. Diversity, then, is characterized as personal, embodied, and derived from the narratives of experience shaped by the particulars of the individual, family dynamics, historical factors, and social, cultural, and political contexts—all of which are crucial to place-based education also. The relationship is more complex than just knowing place or diversity; as John Dewey (1934) distinguishes—there is a difference between *seeing* and *recognizing* (pp. 52, 53). Seeing requires sustained attention to the qualities present in situations; it is exploratory in character.

Recognition is the act of assigning a label or classification; once categorized, exploration ceases. Dewey (1934) talks of common patterns within his notion of *experience*, commenting that there are conditions to be met without which experience cannot come to be. Perhaps these recursive patterns constitute the needed space (Dewey's conditions) for diversity. In creating curriculum through language, I agree with Michael Kreyling (2001) when he writes that to "keep the conversation going, and keep it balanced between the artefactual and non-artefactual realities," is necessary to understand diversity along with the "projects that have created, indicted, refurbished, or rebirthed it" (p. 18). In curriculum, reflection and action feed one another; collectively they make curriculum a process, and as faculty we are in it, body and mind.

Teaching is lived as it transpires; the participants must be responsible for the creation of the program alongside the architects. Lived spaces, as William Schubert (2003) states, "need to move beyond *places* in which we live out our scholarly lives to reflect more fully on *places* that our scholarly ponderings influence and should influence" (p. ii). Place-based social justice should evolve into a set of experiences that attempts to inspire the notion of *educators as change agents*, seeking to liberate students through reflection and action, thereby living out theory in practice (Freire, 1970/1997). Freirean (1970/1997) dialogue of democratic creation becomes fundamental in which teachers and students work together to perceive *difference* as a driving force in education and examine the moral complexities of diversity (Milligan 2001). We are troubled by the "lack of place" within traditional curricula for creating the conditions for *extraordinary politics* that might enable an education about diversity to become a movement for diversity (Euchner, 1996). However, there is hope for change. Hannah Arendt's (1958) conception of *plurality* (as moments of rupture, displacement, and dislocation in history) enable students to recover potentials lost in the past so that they may find actualization in their present. Arendt (1958) identifies plurality, the fundamental nature of being human such that "nobody is ever the same as anyone else who ever lived, lives, or will live" as "the condition of human action" (p. 7). Arendt (1958) explains that those deprived of seeing and hearing others, of being seen and heard by others "are all imprisoned in the subjectivity of their own singular experience, which does not cease to be singular if the same experience is multiplied innumerable times ... seen only under one aspect and is permitted to present itself in only one perspective" (p. 58).

· 6 ·

CURRICULUM AS TRANSACTIONAL AESTHETIC

The success of a revolution lies only in itself, precisely the vibrations, the embraces and the openings that it gave to human beings at the time of their happening and that make up a monument which is constantly evolving, like those tumuli to which each new visitor brings a stone.

—GILLES DELEUZE AND FÉLIX GUATTARI

In bringing together rather than separating the diverse poles of philosophy and social sciences, critical theory sought to uncover the "circumstances that enslave" humans (Horkheimer, 1982, p. 244) while also creating practical approaches to the issues of the day. As Douglas Kellner (2003) noted, critical theory built upon Hegelian notions of critique by "criticizing one-sided positions...and developing more complex dialectal perspectives" (p. 52). In his own work, Kellner sought to bring together multiple narratives in pursuit of overarching concepts that guide, inspire, and proliferate. As we consider education, we might well follow Kellner's lead by appropriating his "meta-theoretical" concept on critical theory. Within this cover, we find room to link theory to practice in the everyday experiences of educators and students. Also, in applying a metatheoretical approach, we find ample opportunity to approach curriculum as a richly embossed text, as yet unfinished. Within this chapter, we hope to contribute to the unfolding curricular narrative with specific emphasis given to the fundamental elements required for an aesthetic education. We hope to build on thoughts from the previous chapter that positioned education as an aesthetic experience capable of enlivening the senses and re-awakening a sense of self within community.

Indeed, from our perspective, the metaphor of curriculum as a text presents a means to engage in the conversations and the dialogical processes that help educators and learners alike amend, and in significant ways mend the educational narrative. More importantly, the narrative, as it constructed and reconstructed, is neatly couched within the confines of community that sustains and benefits from conversations. In short, we seek to explore the idiosyncratic moment that offers the opportunity to co-create the structures necessary for a "lived connection" to education and to the future beyond school-based learning. An aesthetic education, in short, is an integrated curricular text that emphasizes transactional experiences that are situated within an environment that makes life possible and more importantly, meaningful. These transactional curricula place renewed importance on play, curiosity, exploration, self-reflective practices, and intentional ambiguity—all elements missing from contemporary schooling and all elements to which we shall return later.

Reading the multiple texts of schooling, we see a hermeneutic inconsistency that plagues education and which disallows the connections between individuals, content, and place-based idioms that foster change and which lead toward the aesthetic moment. We can also see that the de-focused emphasis on collecting isolated and related artifact, or content knowledge, represents the primary focus of schooling. In large part, insistence upon content knowledge rather than critical and autonomous thinking stems from the rise of modernity and its emphasis on evidence and categorization (Leppert, 2004) as well as from the industrial age and its need for workers who followed strict protocol in factories. In these contexts, questioning, critical thinking, and autonomous actions (all part of what a good education should encourage) are not only frowned upon, but actively discouraged.

The once richly colored parchment, on which the text of schooling was written, with many chapters and multiple voices, has now been white washed, leaving little room for improvisation and imagination. In the place of play, curiosity, and exploration, curricula have become the recitation of facts, figures, and dates. In the place of localized meaning, national dictates, much like medical doctors, prescribe clinical interventions that treat symptoms but often not the underlying causes of illness. And although reform movements often captured the tone and tenor of the times, when seen as a whole, they seem mainly to have played upon national fears and sharp shifts in national demographics to deepen the connections between learning, economic and military potential, and career management. With only rare exceptions, accountability movements re-emphasized a mind-numbing insistence on distributed "truths," curricula that come alive with place-based meaning and intimate connections to the lived experiences of individuals not simply marginalized, but rather eradicated from the educational landscape.

While the lines between education, national security, and job training have been largely blurred, what remains clear is the myriad of discarded curricular carcasses that once seemed promising but which never met their lofty goals. As political winds blew from right to left, opportunists joined their plain talk about education and the future of the United States with rampant public paranoia that often saw the imminent decline of the nation through the lens of falling test scores on international exams and the achievements of other countries. In a nation that sees education as the primary means to civic engagement, socio-economic equality, and maintenance of Super Power status, educational failure fostered an existential questioning of self that promoted the rise of an educational hegemony bent on restoring the meaning of being American. Too often, however, curricular reforms were not only attached to the flavor-of-the-day movements, but were also held captive to politically motivated and inorganic reforms. Over time, the result was curricula situated within a concentrated sense of place that disregarded the multiplicities of spaces within those places.

It might be convenient to position the collapsing of the curriculum to the late 20th century, and more specifically with the 1983 publication of A Nation at Risk, its origins, however, date to a much earlier time. Large-scale control of schooling began in earnest with Horace Mann's attempts, in Massachusetts, to establish the Common School. Although each school maintained a modicum of independence, the defining characteristics were an emphasis on the "three Rs" (reading, [w]riting, and [a]rithmetic) as well as end-of-year recitations that provided grades and some measure of accountability for parents. In spite of Mann's best efforts, following his death, the Common School movement fizzled under the weight of its challenge and push from parochial schools to determine their own, localized curricula (Cremin, 1980; Kaestle, 1983; & Katz, 2012). Still, Mann's troubling legacy, as Bob Pepperman Taylor (2010) notes, resounds fully today. Mann's insistence of moral certainly and political consensus over questioning and intellectual curiosity condemned schooling to a mere shadow of its potential. Channeling

Mann, President Calvin Coolidge clearly called for political and educational consensus on the future and meaning of America. Speaking to the American Society of Newspaper editors in 1925, President Coolidge, in a staunch defense of business, noted that "After all, the chief business of the American people is business" (American Presidency Project). Coolidge, however, did not stop there. He insisted that any attempts to criticize business and businessmen were ill-founded and harmful. And, in an interesting first annunciation of trickle-down economic theory, he noted that "Wealth is the product of industry, ambition, character and untiring effort. In all experience, the accumulation of wealth means the multiplication of schools, the increase of knowledge, the dissemination of intelligence, the encouragement of science, the broadening of outlook, the expansion of liberties, the widening of culture." (American Presidency Project).

While Coolidge tied education to economic growth, it was the Cold War and Soviet successes in math and science, epitomized by the 1957 launch of Sputnik that created direct connections between education and national security. Such well-known figures as Admiral Hyman Rickover (1959/1963) suggested that the progressive education movement, spearheaded by John Dewey, had laid the foundations for national failure and had put the nation at risk of falling to the Soviet Union. Rickover and others argued that only by returning to the fundamentals of education, to the basics of drill and memorization, and to the commitment of facts to memory, could an educational restoration occur (Ravitch, 1983). The American public's fear of Soviet dominance, the lingering effects of Sputnik, and outrage over the supposed "spoon feeding" taking place in American schools led directly to presidential action and the passage of the National Defense Education Act (NDEA) of 1958. This bi-partisan legislative action sought to strengthen math and science education (as well as language learning) in pursuit of a national security agenda.

Fast forward 34 years and another report on American schools, A Nation at Risk, once again provoked public outrage at the perceived failures of the educational system. Bold and contentious language, including "the educational foundations of our society are presently being eroded by a rising tide of mediocrity that threatens our very future as a Nation" and the assertion that "If an unfriendly foreign power had attempted to impose on America the mediocre educational performance that exists today, we might well have viewed it as an act of war" (A Nation at Risk), were scattered throughout the report and served to mobilize reform-minded politicians. Calling for not only a return to the basics, but also pathways toward creating skilled workers ready for the challenges of the coming millennium, A Nation at Risk ushered in an era of accountability that remains firmly in place.

By the late 20th century it became clear that the streams of educational reform converged into a mighty torrent that combined national (in)security and job training in the service of economic development. By merging Coolidge's insistence that business is the foundation of the country and fears of Cold War foes or faceless terrorists, politicians wove narratives of dread and defeat into educational programs that have come and gone with each new administration.

More often than not, however, George W. Bush's No Child Left Behind (NCLB) educational initiative, with good reason, has served as the primary piñata for those who decry the move toward accountability and standardization. Under NCLB, states were ostensibly given flexibility. It came, however, with a price. As Congressman Cass Ballenger noted, "the bill takes a two-track approach, expanding flexibility for States and local school districts while holding them strictly accountable for increasing student achievement" (House of Representatives, 2001). While the goals of NCLB, including closing the achievement gap, creating equal opportunities for all children, and raising proficiency in reading, are certainly laudable, many of those early objectives were lost in the emphasis on assessment and accountability.

As Barack Obama entered office in early 2009, many expected that an era of change had arrived. Yet, on July 24, 2009, when Obama and Education Secretary Arne Duncan announced the Race to the Top (R2T) initiative, educators realized that plus ça change, plus c'est la même chose.[1] Accountability, assessment, and a new emphasis on a national curriculum, the Common Core Learning Standards (CCLS), pervaded the reforms and concretized many, if not most, of the Bush-era policies. Obama and Duncan capitalized on the ongoing fear of deterioration of American education and pointed to the results of the 2009 Program for International Student Assessment (PISA), "an international assessment that measures 15-year-old students' reading, mathematics, and science literacy." PISA "also includes measures of general or cross-curricular competencies, such as problem solving" (http://nces.ed.gov/surveys/pisa) as proof. Indeed, Duncan noted that on international assessments of critical areas, the United States is often 23rd or 24th, an unacceptable level of educational failure.[2] He added that "We can quibble, or we can face the brutal truth that we're being out-educated" (Why the Common Core/Sarah Garland/huffingtonpost.com/2013/10/15/

why-common-core_n_4102763.html). To remedy the serious malaise in education, the Obama administration worked closely with the National Governors Association and the Council of Chief State School Officers to promote and create the CCLS, a collection of standards that "provide a clear understanding of what students are expected to learn, so teachers and parent know what they need to do to help them" and which "are designed to be robust and relevant to the real world, reflecting the knowledge and skills that our young people need for success in college an careers" (Common Core: State Standards Initiative).

Supporters and detractors alike had much to say about the CCLS. For those who championed the standards, they pointed to the CCLS's potential to improve education through the implementation of strict standards and testing, to flagging test results on international assessments, including PISA and Trends in International Mathematics and Science Study (TIMSS), and to the promise of correcting the accountability problems from the NCLB program. And finally, many CCLS enthusiasts also pointed to the almost universal adoption (45 states, plus the District of Columbia[3]) as recognition of serious need for improvement in teaching and learning as well as the validity of the standards.

Early on, at the launch of the CCLS, Duncan's tone was both enthusiastic and collaborative. He noted that "As the nation seeks to maintain our international competiveness, ensure all students regardless of background have access to a high quality education, and prepare all students for college, work, and citizenship...these standards are an important foundation for our collective work"(Garland). However, as opposition to the CCLS grew, Duncan's defense of the Obama administration's educational reform initiatives seemed to become increasingly hostile. By 2013, Duncan had taken to categorizing opponents to R2T and the CCLS as fringe elements motivated by "political silliness" (National Press Club, Sept 30, 2013) and overly concerned about "really wacky stuff: mind control, robots, and biometric brain mapping" (speech to newspaper editors in June 2013, Garland).

In mid-November 2013, Duncan continued his poorly articulated defense of the administration's educational policies during a speech to a group of school superintendents in Richmond, Virginia. While no stranger to controversy and misplaced remarks, including his suggestions that Hurricane Katrina was "the best thing that happened to the education system in New Orleans," Secretary Duncan, in preparing his comments, could not have anticipated the swiftly approaching controversy. Speaking to these educators, Duncan defended the

CCLS and more specifically the testing regime that accompanies them by claiming that some of the backlash against the standards comes from white suburban moms. In rather clumsy phrasing, Duncan suggested that "It's fascinating to me that some of the pushback is coming from, sort of, white suburban moms who—all of a sudden—[realize] their child isn't as brilliant as they thought they were and their school isn't quite as good as they thought they were, and that's pretty scary" (first reported by Politco.com). Within hours, social media were in a frenzy as Duncan's statements were tweeted, texted, and emailed across the nation. Although Duncan did his best to control damage by semi-apologizing for what he called "clumsy" remarks, the incident renewed focus on the CCLS and the Obama's administration's Race to the Top (R2T).

While Duncan defended, others were offended. The CCLS's emphasis on improving education through the implementation of strict standards and testing resonates well with a large segment of the population. However, many people remained concerned by what they consider the federalization of education. Duncan's answers during House of Representatives hearings in spring 2009 only fueled fear of a federal takeover of education. In May 2009, Duncan made it explicitly clear that what "NCLB got fundamentally wrong is they were very, very loose on the goals. So you have 50 states, 50 different goal posts, all over the map" (The Obama Administration's Educational Agenda, 2009, p. 96). Nationalization of curriculum, or what Duncan considered substitution of strong federal guidelines for weak state standards, was at the heart of R2T and the CCLS. However, pointing to the 1965 passage of the Elementary and Secondary Education Act (ESEA) opponents challenged the federal government's right to impose federal standards on states. This act, renewed every five years since initial passage, prevented the federal government from directing and/or controlling public education, including curriculum and teaching materials.

Opponents of the CCLS also draw attention to the decay of local control of curriculum. In particular, they point to the case of New York State, one of the early adopters of the CCLS. New York Education Commissioner, John King, joined Duncan's defense of the CCLS by calling resistance on the part of special interest groups a co-opting of the standards for ideological reasons. Channeling Duncan's inappropriate language, King went so far as to liken resistance to the Montgomery Bus Boycott, insinuating that all who oppose the reforms are little more than segregationists dressed as caring parents (Strauss & Burris, 2013). Beyond King's ill-informed and inflammatory comments, under his leadership, New York seems to have gone beyond simple "standards."

As an example, the following excerpt from New York's massive (339 pages) Common Core Mathematics Curriculum provides rather strict guidelines for teachers:

Classwork[4]

Example 1 (20 minutes)

Show the first 1:08 minutes of video below, telling the class that our goal will simply be to describe the motion of the man in words. (Note: Be sure to stop the video at 1:08 because after that the answers to the graphing questions are given.)

Elevation vs. Time #2 [http://www.mrmeyer.com/graphingstories1/graphingstories2.mov. This is the second video under "Download Options" at the site http://blog.mrmeyer.com/?p=213 called "Elevation vs. Time #2."]

After viewing the video, have students share out loud their ideas on describing the motion. Some might speak in terms of speed, distance traveled over time, or change of elevation. All approaches are valid. Help students begin to shape their ideas with precise language.

Direct the class to focus on the change of elevation of the man over time and begin to put into words specific details linking elevation with time.

"How high do you think he was at the top of the stairs? How did you estimate that elevation?"

"Were there intervals of time when his elevation wasn't changing? Was he still moving?"

"Did his elevation ever increase? When?"

Help students discern statements relevant to the chosen variable of elevation

The direct scripting of teacher actions contradicts King's assurances that that the CCLS represent only a general curricular framework rather than a "canned curriculum" that replaces teacher autonomy and place-based education with state-approved lessons. The scripting of classroom materials, often labeled as "teacher proof," is reminiscent of *Man: A Course of Study* (MACOS), a popular 1960s teaching program based on Jerome Bruner's educational theories. However, significant and importance differences are clear. In MACOS, students were actively encouraged to make connections between disparate elements of the curriculum, to ask questions, and to reach conclusions from evidentiary and logical stances. In the example of scripted teaching from the State of New York, few, if any, of these qualities are present. Students are expected to answer scripted questions that might or might not be relevant to their developmental levels.

Regardless of the push and pull over educational reform, the role of standards in education, and the quarrel over "national v. local" authority, the political focus on the perceived failure of schools to teach job skills and provide programs that help keep the nation secure, resonates with the general public. Story after story of failing schools and incompetent teachers permeate the mainstream media. Families worry about the future of their children. The nation worries about its very survival. Through powerful public relations mechanisms, the federal government has convinced a weary and scared public that education has failed and that the only answers come in the form of intervention and accountability.

In thinking about the restriction of education in the United States, we would be remiss not to mention demographic changes as an equal partner with hyperbolic debates. Indeed, demographic changes over the past 100 years have also played an important role in changing the landscape on which political and educational activities unfold. Tellingly, the growth of the industrial and then corporate eras resulted in the rapid depopulation of rural areas. From 1900 to 1990 the U.S. population grew from slightly over 76 million to almost 250 million. By 2012, the United States had added more than 60 million additional people, reaching a population of 313 million (U.S. Census Bureau). While these growth rates are impressive, distribution of this growth between urban, suburban, and rural areas adds another important element to understanding curricular reform movements. In 1900, the rural population of the U.S. stood at 72% (U.S. Census Bureau, 2010). By 2010, only 100 years later, the rural-urban population distribution had more than flipped. Urban and their closely attached suburban units, what the U.S. Census Bureau has taken to calling "combined statistical areas," e.g., Washington and Baltimore, now account for 84% of the total U.S. population. Data from the most recent census (2010) suggest that rather than slowing, the trend continues to accelerate. Indeed, from 2000 to 2010, metro areas grew by 11% at the expense of the center of the country and particularly the Great Plains region.

Largely emanating from shifts in centers of population but also influenced by efficiency models that emerged as part of the industrialization process, the number of school districts in the U.S. slipped from more than 127,000 in the early 20th century to just under 14,000 in 2009 (Digest of Education Statistics, 2010). Although the desire for efficiency seemed to fuel the march toward consolidation, the expected economies of scale never seem to materialize. As an example, by 1980, the height of school consolidations, per pupil spending, even after adjusting for inflation, had risen nearly ten fold from 1920. While some of the increased spending can be accounted for by state and federal mandates imposed upon schools, the overall economies of scale, except in a few specific cases, when very small districts are consolidated into larger ones, have not been as widely seen as anticipated (Andrews, Duncombe, & Yinger, 2007),

The consolidation of school districts, while following national trends toward consolidation of population, also provided opportunities to wrest control of schooling from local school boards. Although school funding remains largely the responsibility of individual states (48% of total budget) and local districts (43% of total budget), the impact that federal funds have on large districts has become influential in determining educational priorities. When coupled with punitive aspects of failed NCLB and R2T policies, local school districts are largely beholden to distanced state and federal governments for not only direction, but also their lives.

In this rather untenable scenario, states and schools face several debilitating yet necessary compromises. In the constant search for solutions to economic woes, states and schools are forced to accept the mandates imposed by the federal government. While the impossible Lake Wobegon goals of NCLB policies have been widely proclaimed (100% proficiency in math and reading) and the economic blackmail widely denounced, provisions under the Obama administration's R2T are equally or, according to Diane Ravitch, even more coercive. With more than $5 billion in federal funds up for competition, schools and school districts are now required to evaluate the effectiveness of teachers through flawed instruments of high stakes testing. What is clear is that the importance of education has taken a backseat to the importance of testing. Perhaps more insidiously, the quixotic quest for rising test scores has had the pernicious effects of replacing classroom creativity and place-specific educational goals with curricula and lessons based on test preparation, creating a disequilibrium within the school where tests are rather meaningless to students but of paramount importance to administrators and teachers. This has motivated some, as in the recent cheating scandal in the Atlanta Public Schools, to seek any means, including illegal ones, to demonstrate rising test scores in an effort to maintain school funding and personal perks.

The rapid urbanization of the American population and the concomitant centralization of schools into relatively few districts would seem to suggest a creeping homogeneity of schools, pupils, and communities, and would perhaps suggest a warranted move to national curricula. Yet, even a cursory glance at the landscape discounts any notion of specific commonalities. Even within distinct and sometimes small areas, levels of income, race, gender, political affiliations and a plethora of other differences are noteworthy. Unfortunately, the intuitive assignment of meaning to specific spaces rests, as Akhil Gupta (1995) notes, on the spatial proximity of the "other" and ignores the ways in which borders are formed, deformed, and eventually reformed in a discursive socio-political act. The other, in a sense, occupies an adjacent territory that is distinct in character. This concept ignores both the morphological aspects of space and the ways in which spaces converge and overlap in various ways. To combat assigned and fixed identities, or the territorialization of meaning, we turn to multi-scalar geography and the avenues of understanding deterritorialization that it offers. In short, a look at space through this lens demonstrates the myriad of ways in which borders overlap along political, socio-economic, and other phenomena. In so doing, a complex and deeply contoured spatial model emerges that draws connections instead of imposing spurious divisions. The complicated and textured discourses among and between the inhabitants of these richly diverse places is only flattened by a common educational curriculum that includes high stakes and punitive testing and, more often than not, failure.

Turning from the narrowly conceived notions which ground contemporary curricular reforms and which fail to create the sparks which inspire self-reflection and which foster persistence, we can begin writing our aesthetic curriculum on the rich and deeply textured parchment of a place-based education. In contrast to stale, mind-numbing, and pernicious conceptualization of schooling as the means of cultural transmission (Apple, 1996; Bourdieu & Passerson, 1977), we propose a look at a means of considering aesthetics within education that reframes the sense of aesthetics within its original Greek meaning of "sense perception" and the more recent notion of "being alive." When seen as the ability to perceive both present realities and future possibilities, aesthetics is fundamentally concerned with the transformative potential that accompanies moments of questioning and self-reflection that portend emotional, social, and intellectual growth. The aesthetic curriculum, then, awakens the senses across and between all disciplines and challenges rule-bound notions of education that ignore both space and place as determining factors in the lived conditions of individuals and whole communities. In short, we view an aesthetic education as one that offers meaningful and pregnant possibilities to students, teacher, and communities.

The aesthetic curriculum is dependent upon several vital and interlocking elements. Fundamentally, however, a place-based must provide integrated and coherent experiences that are linked in service to a fundamental goal—self-reflection. Currently, curricula exist as a broad collection of courses that creates the illusion of breadth of study at the expense of coherence and meaning. The cafeteria-style approach to learning "fails to provide students with the academic experiences, understood as significant knowledge, critical thinking skills" and intellectual autonomy that are central to education (White, 2010, p. 8). In place of disconnected curricula, we propose integrated programs that are developmentally appropriate, spiraled, and connected across disciplines. Within an aesthetic curriculum, teachers function as guides who gently encourage learners to explore ideas, consider alternatives, and critically evaluate issues. All told, connections between multiple disciplines and emphasis on autonomy rather than restatements of "truths," help students acquire the dispositions to behave as self-reflective and autonomous agents in their own lives and communities.

An aesthetic curriculum must also be place-based as it draws its connections to the lives of individuals from the meaningful interactions they have in daily encounters with common experiences. Some might protest that the daily experiences of many youths are impoverished and lacking in both importance and a connection to mainstream American values. Poverty in its various forms, e.g., economic, educational, cultural, is not a learning disability. Nor does it lessen the value of those who experience it. The lived conditions of individuals are the foundational texts on which their lives are lived, whether in advantaged suburbs or rat-infested tenements. In fact, these experiences provide the sensory data that connect individuals to communities and meaning to education. Further, it is these connections to locality which encourage learners to participate as engaged citizens in their communities while also considering how their micro-communities are part of, impacted by, and related to larger contexts.

In addition, place-based education offers pathways to overcome the debilitating effects of a lack of social capital. When low socio-economic status meets with other educational disadvantages, e.g., race, gender, and ethnicity, nationalized curricula present hard to overcome obstacles that serve, more often than not, as the platform on which self-blame occurs. A place-based curriculum, on the other hand, offers students the opportunity to overcome these barriers through learning experiences that are connected to their everyday lives and their lived conditions. In this way, an aesthetic education does not ignore social and socio-economic injustice. It does not remain deaf to the sirens that cut through the calm night air of so many ravaged American cities. It does not remain unmoved by the bankruptcy of long forgotten promises of equality. It does not remain mute to the challenges of the day. It does not pretend that education, by itself, is the medicine that will alleviate poverty and marginalization. An aesthetic education does not succumb to the popular American myth that hard work and intelligence, when combined, ensure success. Rather, as a descendent of critical theory, an aesthetic education attempts to expose the fundamental power dynamics on which continuation of asymmetric social and economic status is based. It also opens new understandings of the institutional discourses used in the hallways and backrooms of "public" institutions. Let us be sure, however, to realize that an aesthetic education does, alone, ensure instant change in well-entrenched political structures. Indeed, no single institution can accomplish that. However, an aesthetic education works, as with Jacques Rancière's concept of *dissensus*, to promote ongoing incremental change that ultimately challenges the politics of the neo-liberal and neo-conservative state.

The insistence on place in education is not to say that curricula must be so "place heavy" that they ignore broader societal goals. The importance of a literate and civic-minded population that understands democratic practices at the local and national levels is vital to the health of a democracy. Likewise, transferable skills rather than an insistence upon the requirements of local industry helps individuals locate meaningful employment whether in their own neighborhoods or further afield. With this in mind, it is easy to consider the various meanings of community and to return to Jacques Rancière's claim that communities are in a constant state of flux, determined and delineated by micro needs that create macro forces. This view, like multi-scalar geography, suggests that communities are not neat packages with clear boundaries, but rather amorphous entities that grow, shrink, and change shape as they mature. Nonetheless, a basic starting point for education is the idiosyncratic loci in which individuals live, learn, and discover who they are and how they relate to others.

Successful curricula are also dependent upon attention to the importance of play and curiosity. Although the preparation for standardized testing has caused an over reliance on direct instructional techniques, researchers, including Lev Vygotsky (1967; 1978) as well as Hirsh-Pasek and Golinkoff (2003), have long noted the crucial contributions of play in education. These include, among others, reduced stress, better social skills, and improved cognitive abilities. For young children, Vygotsky contended that play helps them use their imagination to "stand a head taller," meaning that play expands potential and engages mental capacities in ways that traditional direct instruction cannot. What is interesting, with regard to place-based learning, is that young children expand and contract their "communities" according to the game. For some, as observed by Deborah Leong (Bodrova & Leong, 2007), national hardware stores and airport security operations form the stage on which play occurs. For others, highly localized and personal contexts are explored, transformed, and understood through play. Whatever form play takes, it is fundamental to fostering imagination and to counteracting the boredom inherent in test-preparation and DIS-placed curricula.

Yet, even with mounting indications that play adds essential elements of education, including interesting avenues for exploration of ideas, language, and community, it is largely missing from schooling. It appears that at least two imposing factors align to de-emphasize play. First, modernity stressed the need for order that was "marked by and defined by an obsession with 'evidence'" and large-scale social integration/organization (Leppert, 2004, p. 13). Play, with its seeming silliness and lack of seriousness, presents a terrifying opposition to the order of schooling and the neatness of lesson plans and curricula. Yet, it is precisely the chaos inherent in play that animates learning opportunities and which lies at the heart of an aesthetic curriculum. Second, schooling and other collections of knowledge, according to Bernice Murphy (2005), engaged in nothing short of a re-organization and control of memory, history, and perhaps most importantly time that was required for regulating and revising history. Murphy (2005) also asserts that "The clock, not the steam engine, is the key-machine of the modern industrial age" (p. 70) in that it divorced time from human events and, in Marxist terms, alienated oppressed social and cultural groups from long-lived patterns of social cooperation and reflexivity. The mathematical and quasi-scientific divisions of time create easily identifiable and compartmentalized periods of history that are problematic and incomplete. Play, with its unpredictable spontaneity, multi-directionality, and chaotic character fits poorly with the dictates of the clock by challenging factory models of education that rely on precise and often scripted lesson plans and exact time management standards.

Increased regimentation and control of time, however attractive and required by industrial societies, lead to a loss of self in society that is rapidly replaced by a sense of collected, catalogued, and forgotten. As time is constrained to a precise and present moment, personal pedagogies and future possibilities are lost. All that remains is a sense of commonality that while attractive denies the reality of differences within society. An aesthetic curriculum, quite to the contrary, would offer the space to explore, to expand, and to evaluate materials based on localized need rather than blind adherence to state or national schedules. By opening the curriculum to the possibilities of discovery, the pernicious effects of standardized testing and lock-step marches toward untenable goals would be eradicated in favor of a "timeless" goal of guiding learners toward self-discovery and the honing of critical thinking skills that help individuals deal with the un-imagined complexities of an increasingly complex world.

And finally, an aesthetic curriculum depends upon self-reflection, or moments of intense cognitive dissonance presented in ambiguous situations. When intentionally linked, these elements create moments of "being alive," with senses a flare and an eagerness for transformation present. Indeed, aesthetics might best be defined as the "fulfillment that comes from awareness of the ways elements of experience interrelate in order to bring about the formation of complex unities that are marked by emergent" and new conceptualizations (Beardsley, 1973, p. 49). These moments are not unlike Lessing's pregnant moment that captures the chaos of a situation and the multiplicity of concurrent events. These moments suggest a sequential narrative that calls each to question what has transpired, what is present, what is about to happen, and perhaps most importantly, what is possible.

Although perhaps troubling, these moments are rooted in a complex understanding of self within a community, whether large or small, as well as the knowledge that only through reflexive activities can one emerge with a more complete appreciation of self. We also note that the purpose of an aesthetic curriculum or an aesthetic experience is not solely episodic. Much like Gilles Deleuze and Félix Guattari (1996), who suggest that the success of a revolution is contingent upon a continuous evolution of the individual and not a single, easily defined instance, an aesthetic education spirals towards new discoveries, new insights, and new ways of becoming that build one on another. An aesthetic education is intentional, powerful, and ongoing!

The elements of an aesthetic education represent a significant departure from schools that have perfected their "training" role and are now the principal site where agreement between public policy and popular will is forged. More importantly, an aesthetic curriculum, working from and through the elements above, opens opportunities for self-reflective and exploratory activities that lead toward the aesthetic moment. An aesthetic curriculum possesses, like Kellner's (2003) metatheoretical concept for critical theory, the broad linkages on which democratic and socially just education can occur. It responds and speaks to individuals who are marginalized in schools and society by reading between the lines and using the community as text. It is communal and connects the problems, challenges, and possibilities found in all communities with the people who inhabit their communities and who are best able to effect change. And finally, it is liberating in ways the current focus on testing and assigning blame for failure to students is not.

Looking back at our curricular text, we find tensions written into the parchment. From the Soviet launch of Sputnik in 1957 to the publication of A Nation at Risk, to present preoccupations with job training, each new American generation has seemingly been met with geo-political crises that warranted government intervention in schools. Yet each new reform move-ment masked important questions of individual and place in education. Although given new names and new faces, each reform shared the common characteristics of maligning the then current state of education without pro-viding significant details on how to make improvement, creating "pathways" to employment, and progressively restricting the curricular distinctions among the nation's 14,000 school districts in an effort to form common learning stan-dards and national assessment regimes.

Yet, reforms have failed to live up to their billing. Headlines in the nation's newspapers and websites still scream Asian Nations Dominate In-ternational Assessment and U.S. Students Lag behind International Peers.[5] The national tragedy of high school dropout rates, not to mention middle- and elementary schools, persists. And, social injustice and hate crimes seem to be on the rise. By almost any surface measure, American schooling has seemed to fail, but not in the ways proponents of assessment and accountability claim. More testing of students and more blame for teachers is not the answer. Prolonged school years with more of the same would not help. Additional remedial classes in math and sciences would only scratch the surface of the national educational malaise. Rather than blaming students and teachers, we must face the challenges head on. From our perspective there is no more daunting task than the realization that American education has not respond-ed to the localized and place-based needs of the many disadvantaged youth in the urban, suburban, and rural areas of the country. With its focus on collec-tivity at the expense of the individual, educational policy has privileged some while marginalizing most. Further, with sanitized assessment narratives lead-ing the way, pedagogy, as we suggested in chapter 3, is largely an interaction-al and prescriptive act visited upon students by carefully "trained" teachers whose conduct is monitored and controlled by others. In place of these anes-thetic and imposed practices, we argue that a transactional pedagogy, based on reflexivity between curriculum and student as well as teacher and learner, best connects individuals to the meaning-making experiences within communities. All of these elements lead to re-emphasizing pedagogies of place that harness the richness and potential of a localized curriculum in the pursuit of the aesthetic moment and the emancipatory potential of unbridled schooling.

As education continues to be restricted to the service of national security and economic growth, we wish to simply add a voice to the conversation that once again calls for a critical approach to learning that focuses on the need to liberate humans "from the circumstances that enslave them" (Horkheimer, 1982, p. 244), a critical plea that is often ignored in the current neo-liberal and neo-conservative dominated environment. For us, these conversations echo above the sound of sirens in our city streets. They are heard over the desperate calls of drug and alcohol addictions in many rural areas. They draw attention to the social injustice found on almost every street corner in American cities. And, they champion the multi-accented world that is true testimony to the power and promise of place in education!

Notes

1. The more things change, the more they stay the same.
2. The PISA was repeated in 2012 with results suggesting that American youths remain far below Asians in math (rank = 36), reading (rank = 24), and science (rank = 28). Arne Duncan remarked that the results suggest "a picture of education stagnation" in the United States.
3. On November 21, 2013, following Secretary of Education Arne Duncan's "suburban mom" comments and mindful of increasing discontent within the state, Louisiana State Superintendent John White announced the state would drop out of the CCLS initiative for at least two years. Louisiana's decision to opt out brought the number of states adopting the standards to 44.
4. This excerpt appears on page 13 of the New York Common Core Mathematics Curriculum.
5. Associated Press (12/5/2013) and the Organization for Economic Cooperation and Development (12/5/2013).

CONCLUSION

The Journey Ahead: Our Radical Ontological Calling as Curriculum Scholars

Our call for considering curriculum as space is predicated upon certain expectations for that space. To the degree that space provides opportunities for authentic existential and intellectual journeys, then curriculum as space supports *currere*. Yet, in the heterotopia of educational reform, we must acknowledge the role of power in producing contested spaces in which teachers, students, and communities themselves must exist. As such, we must seek justice alongside authenticity. Our work is always political. Our work is always moral (Dewey, 1959; Pinar, 2001; Purpel & McLaurin, 2004).

Throughout this book we have attempted to create Foucault's heterotopic mirror, drawing you into a complicated conversation situated between reality and the ideal. However, unlike some theoretical texts, we have challenged you to engage—to act upon your discomfort. We ask that you let go of your fears, anxieties, assumptions, and your need for control in order to enter into yet unknown spaces as part of a collective body. This requires the equivalent of a full-moon ritual of release and renewal. Burke (2001) describes this release as she chronicles her experience helping her partner Joan die. She shares,

Joan's and my last dance together spun her into a spiral of light and back into the arms of the universe. It pushed me into a contemplative and reflective time, feeling the enormous loss while sensing her amazing liberation. She accepted death as a transformation and a rebirthing process. Our six months of seclusion and uninterrupted care was an unusual articulation of political and feminist activism (p. 75).

By engaging ritual in a critical part of her life, Burke notes that she was able to see things she would not otherwise expect. By changing her consciousness about the cycle of life, she was able to change her reality. Even so, Burke recognizes that this existential journey alongside her partner, even through death, was also political. Who Joan and Betty were in life was shaped by the social and historical spaces they occupied. Like Betty, we must release ourselves in order to engage with one another, in order to embrace our historical connections and live together as exiles (Sennett, 1994). Thus, we must be wide awake and engaged with the contested spaces we occupy, and we must engage our moral and cosmopolitan imaginations to act upon those spaces.

In order to shift our thinking into Popper's (1984/1992) critical world, we need to seek out contested spaces and challenge ourselves to see differently within those spaces. To this end, we offer three aesthetic encounters: three complicated conversations enacted within contested spaces found in films. These three spaces personify the intersections between the political and the existential. They reinforce the reality that we cannot rest within introspection manifested exclusively in philosophical prose. Instead, we must simultaneously let go and reach out. We begin with a space that is subject to contested politics and power. No Man's Land takes place in a supposed neutral zone between warring Bosnians and Serbians, and it painfully demonstrates how all spaces are contested and complicated. We then explore another politically contested space, Kandahar, but we examine it through a stronger existential lens—through the eyes of Nefas. Finally, we end with an image of hope. We examine a small Appalachian community during the early 1900s as a teacher, Dr. Lily Penleric, tries to capture the mountain music of supposedly simple mountain folk in order to study its European roots.

Contested Political Space: *No Man's Land*

This 2001 film written and directed by Danis Tanović was set during the Bosnian and Serbian war. Two soldiers from opposing sides find themselves in the middle ground, the "no man's land" between the two enemy lines. There is a third soldier in the space as well, a Bosnian whose body was placed on top of a live land mine while he was unconscious. The movie focuses on the two soldiers caught in this space. At times they are hurling threats and insults at one another and at other times they recognize everyday ways in which their lives literally and figuratively intersect. At times in these "neutral" trenches, either Čiki, the Bosnian soldier, or Nino, the Serbian soldier, get control of the one gun. When this happens, the one holding the gun flaunts his power over the other.

This space in the trenches is juxtaposed with the larger context and the influence of the United Nations Protection Force (UNPROFOR). This force, led by the French sergeant Marchand, attempts to intervene and save the three men. They are forced to deal with opposition from the UNPROFOR leadership as well as from the Bosnian and the Serbian forces. Captain DuBois of the UN High Command argues that they should not deal with the men caught in the middle:

> You can't expect me to risk the lives of our soldiers in order to save theirs, can you? I hope that I don't have to remind you, Captain, of the precise purpose of our mission here in Bosnia... I don't think that the General Assembly of the UN is going to convene itself specifically in order to deal with the problems of two unknown individuals trapped in no man's land... tell them, as usual, that neither side can agree.

To those in power outside the trenches, particularly those watching the conflict between the Bosnians and the Serbs from the sidelines, the men in the trenches were collateral damage—the price they paid for their perceived and safe engagement. To further complicate matters, teams of reporters and photographers have come to report the event.

Both spaces are rife with conflict and complexity. The two young soldiers at times fully embrace the adversarial roles to which they have been assigned and at other, albeit brief, moments, they experience sparks of doubt and recognition that, though enemies, they are connected through common acquaintances and similar experiences. Those potentially cosmopolitan moments are disrupted, however, by their raw emotions regarding the ways in which the war has interrupted their lives and changed them, and they see in the face of the other soldier the cause of the war. In particular, they continually argue, blaming each other for starting the war. Petrunic (2005) analyzes their experiences and how those experiences impact their collective identities:

> Actively identifying with other individuals in their collective identities (Bosnian Muslim or Serbian Orthodox) to fight an ethnic conflict becomes increasingly difficult when Nino and Čiki, as individual identities, engage in moments of recognition

realizing little differentiates one man from another.... The trench as a particular location engages their beings in a hermeneutic play. By sparing the life of the other man, peace is observed—a peace that erupts into war outside the boundaries of the trench (p. 5).

While the one space focuses on the conflict between Čiki and Nino, the other focuses on dysfunctional political systems that perpetuate injustice. Neither the Bosnians nor the Serbs want to get involved. They do not know who exactly is caught between the two sides. The UN forces, once compelled to act, focus their efforts on generating a perception of peace keeping rather than genuine resolution of the conflict. Once the men are rescued from the trench, once they are once again identified as Bosnian and Serbian, they erupt. Čiki shoots Nino first, and then he is shot by a peacekeeper.

The fall-out from the experience does not end with the death of Čiki and Nino. The UN forces determine that they cannot successfully defuse the land mine underneath Cera, the second Bosnian soldier in the trench. However, they cannot risk the media finding out that they are willing to leave a soldier to die inside the trench. They generate a big production that gives the appearance that they are removing the soldier, and the UNPROFOR commander then leaks information to both sides that the other will attempt to reoccupy the trench that night in hopes that both sides will strike and kill Cera along with the evidence that he has been left behind. The film ends with the UN forces, reporters, and cameramen leaving the area and then pans out to see Cera lying there alone and helpless.

Our classrooms function, in many ways, like the trenches of the no man's land. While we may operate as if classrooms and schools and neutral and spared from political forces, they are actually highly contested spaces shaped by political forces and those in power. Aware teachers often struggle with the roles to which they have been assigned, and only the truly courageous challenge the prescribed protocols and the exclusive focus on measured accountability. Scholars, for the most part, remain complicit—failing to uncover the false perceptions of success that are advertised over mass media outlets and commodified through large textbook publishing companies and consultant gigs. Figuratively speaking, we look down at Cera and feel helpless. Yet, as Freire (1998) admonished years ago, if we see injustice and turn away, then we are immoral. Concurring with Freire, Helfenbein (2004) asks us to rethink power relationships through a radicalized space where we "not only understand the landscape and the social and cultural processes that create it [spaces], but also allow for the impact of individuals upon the terrain put before them" (71).

We must accept our radical ontological vocation of being in the world full of conflict and engage that world in spite of our fears and frustrations.

Contested Identities: *Kandahar*

This 2001 film was set in Afghanistan. It is based upon an Afghan refugee woman's attempt to save a childhood friend who plans to kill herself. In the movie, Nafas, a woman who was born in Afghanistan but who escaped to Canada when she was ten years old, has returned to Afghanistan in hopes of saving her sister. As a child, her sister reached for a doll that had been rigged with a bomb and she lost both of her legs. Now that their father has died, this sister wrote to Nafas and told her that she will kill herself at the next lunar eclipse. Nafas is able to enter Afghanistan with the help of the Red Cross, but from that point on she must find her own way to reach Kandahar. As she journeys, she records her thoughts on a tape recorder. She tells the Red Cross pilot that it is her own "black box," in case she does not return. She begins by posing as a fourth wife in a family of travelers. Shortly after they begin their journey to Kandahar, however, they are attacked by thieves and lose all their money and possessions. The family chooses to return to Iran and leaves Nafas stranded in a small village. While she is there, she encounters a young boy, Khak, whom she pays to accompany her. At one point Khak sings for Nafas to record for her sister. She then records this message:

> I'm collecting everything to give you hope, like the voice of this young boy. Can the boys still sing songs in the alley ways of Kandahar? Can the girls still fall in love with those songs? Does love exist through the covering of the burka?

When Nafas falls ill, Khak takes her to an African American doctor who came to Afghanistan years before and who now poses as a Middle Easterner offering medical aid within a small village. He came to Afghanistan in search of God and fought first with the Soviets and then with various tribal factions. As Nafas recovers, the doctor takes her closer to Kandahar, dropping her off at the Red Cross clinic for amputees. As he prepares to leave her, he asks if he can do anything else. Nafas asks him to record a message of hope for her sister. He responds,

> You know, a person needs a reason for living, and in difficult circumstances, hope is that reason. Of course, it's abstract—but for the thirsty it's water. For the hungry, it's bread. For the lonely, it's love. For a woman living under full cover, hope is the day she will be seen. How is that? Did you like that? I didn't like it. May I have that (the tape recorder) and try it on my own?

Nafas' final guide is a man who has lost a hand. He is someone who tries to steal legs from the amputee clinic to sell on the black market. Nafas pays him to take her to Kandahar, and to do this he disguises both of them as women in a wedding party. They make it to the edge of Kandahar where they are stopped by a Taliban checkpoint. The soldiers detain her one-handed guide and begin to question her. From this point at the end of the film, the camera angle shifts to see what Nafas sees in the distance: the eclipse of the sun.

Kandahar represents *currere*—the journey we each must take and how we are not only defined by those spaces but also how we are limited by the ways in which those spaces define us. In spite of having escaped the Taliban rule and growing up in Canada, Nafas had to don a burqa in order to travel to save her sister. Further, she could not travel alone. She had to be accompanied by a man, and each man who helps her is marginalized from the Afghan society in one way or another. Weber (2005) explores the implications of this in her analysis of the film:

> The place and placelessness of Afghanistan become the symbolic spatial terrain negotiated by the film's characters. Crisscrossing *Kandahar*'s landscapes, none of them has a stable place. Indeed, all the characters we meet are not only in motion. They are out of place... (p. 363)

This aesthetic encounter leaves us with harsh images that challenge the very core of our cosmopolitan imaginations: girls circling new beautiful dolls to build up a resistance to the temptation of picking it up: learning that doing so will lead to death or dismemberment as the dolls are wired to explosives. In another scene, you see limbs attached to parachutes falling out of the sky and Afghans rushing, many of whom are using shovels and sticks as crutches to maintain their balance, to grab one of these precious commodities in hope of feeling whole again. Throughout the film we struggle with the manner in which girls and women are treated. In the doctor's clinic they must remain behind a veil with a small opening through which the doctor examines them. While wives and daughters of the first family wore beautiful jewelry and painted their nails and wore lipstick, all was hidden beneath the burqas. These raw images of humanity compel us to hold fast with our gaze and recognize how we are connected to a life so very different from our own. It challenges us to recognize the ways in which the spaces we inhabit shape who we are, and it calls us to enter into strange spaces and take on difficult journeys in order to reach those who have lost hope. As the film ends, you hear Nafas' last message to her sister, "I'd always escaped from jails that imprisoned Afghan women. But now I'm a captive in every one of those prisons. Only for you, my sister."

Hope in Contested Spaces: *Songcatcher*

The final aesthetic encounter we introduce is *Songcatcher*, a 2000 film directed by Maggie Greenwald. The film is set in the early 1900s, and the main character is Dr. Lily Penleric, a professor of musicology. After being denied a promotion at her university, Dr. Penleric decides to visit her sister, Eleanor, who is teaching in a small school in the Appalachian Mountains of North Carolina. While visiting, Lily discovers that much of the mountain music she hears is actually traditional English ballads preserved by the seclusion of the mountains. Securing recording devices from her university, Lily travels through the mountains and collects these songs from the people who live there. Over time you see Lily transformed from being the disconnected researcher using the people to advance her knowledge to being a part of the community. She takes on the role of mother for an orphan, Deladis Slocumb. She helps deliver a baby for a woman whose husband has abandoned her. She helps the woman support her children by sending the woman's artwork to the city to be sold in local galleries. Finally, she falls in love with a mountain man, Tom Bledsoe.

The climax of the film occurs when, after seeing Eleanor in a compromising position with the other female teacher in the school, two men in the community set fire to the schoolhouse. All of Lily's recordings and transcripts are destroyed in the fire. After the initial shock of her loss, Lily takes Deladis and Tom down off the mountain in order to build a life in the city. She wants to share the mountain music with the people there in hopes that the world will see the beauty of the mountains and help preserve mountain culture by protecting the land from the encroaching mining companies. As they begin their journey down the mountain, Lily runs into another professor coming to collect the songs that Lily had worked so hard to collect. He asks her to stay and work with him, and she makes the decision to give up her research and build a very different life with Deladis and Tom.

Lily's journey is a prophetic one (Garrison, 1997). While she began her visit to the mountains intellectually aware of the music theory behind the traditional English ballads and while she understood the significance of how those ballads were preserved among the mountain community, she nevertheless grew into a passionate awareness of the beautiful people that the music represented. She stopped being intellectually complacent, and she became morally engaged. We must likewise seek moral engagement in order to support the transactional work of critical cosmopolitanism. When we are in relationship with one another, then we are able to approximate the ideals of our radical ontological calling.

Conclusion

So, in *Curriculum as Spaces*, we are asking you to likewise come down from the mountain. We ask that you simultaneously hold on to your ideological convictions while you let go and connect to the complex world that surrounds you. We challenge you to join together as temporal, vulnerable, and humble exiles working together to engage our shared cosmopolitan imaginations. As we ask this of you, we recognize that this level of aesthetic and prophetic engagement is highly political. We do not live in neutral spaces. Further, we are formed by those spaces in which we live. In order to re-center our curriculum and engage in meaningful transactional work, we must commit ourselves to both a raised consciousness and engagement with one another. After all, it is up to us to create the kinds of spaces in which we wish to live.

REFERENCES

A Nation at Risk: The Imperative for Educational Reform (1983). Washington, DC: The Commission on Excellence in Education.

Adair Breault, D. (2003). Brutal compassion: A requiem. *Educational Studies, 33*(3), 310–316.

Adams, H. (1971). *Critical theory since Plato.* New York:: Harcourt, Brace, & Jovanovich.

Addams, J. (1905). Address. *National Society for the Promotion of Industrial Education.* New York: The Society.

Adelman, H.S., & Taylor, L. (2006). Mapping a school's resources to improve their use in preventing and ameliorating problems. In C. Franklin, M. B. Harris, & P. Allen-Mears (Eds.), *School social work and mental health workers training and resource manual.* New York: Oxford University Press.

Albers, J. (1965). *Search versus re-search.* Hartford, CT: Trinity College Press.

Anderson, B. (1991). *Imagined communities.* New York: Verso.

Anderson, B. (2006). *Imagined communities: Reflections on the origin and spread of nationalism.* London: Verso Books.

Andrews, M., Duncombe, W., & Yinger, J. (2007). Revisiting economies of size in American education: Are we closer to a consensus? *Economics of Education Review, 21,* 245–262.

Appiah, K. A. (2006). *Cosmopolitanism: Ethics in a world of strangers.* New York: W. W. Norton & Company.

Apple, M. W. (1979). *Ideology and curriculum.* New York: Columbia University Press.

Apple, M.W. (1986). *Teachers and texts.* New York: Routledge.

Apple, M. W. (1996). *Cultural politics and education.* New York: Teachers College Press.

Arendt, H. (1958). *The human condition*. Chicago: University of Chicago Press.

Au, W. (2012). The long march toward revitalization: Developing standpoint in curriculum studies. *Teachers College Record*, 114(5), 1–30.

Ayers, W. (2013). Lesson one: Reverence. In A. G. Rud and J. Garrison's (Eds), *Teaching with reverence: Reviving an ancient virtue for today's schools*. New York: Palgrave Macmillan, 129–136.

Bakhtin, M. (1981). *The dialogical imagination: Four essays*. Austin, TX: University of Texas Press.

Bauman, Z. (2000). *Liquid modernity*. Malden, MA: Polity Press.

Beardsley, M. (1973). What is an aesthetic quality? *Theoria*, 39(1–3), 50–70.

Beardsley, M. (1982). *The aesthetic point of view*. Ithaca, NY: Cornell University Press.

Bennett, D. et al. (Fall 2012). An education for the twenty-first century: Stewardship of the global commons. *Liberal Education*, 98(4). Accessed December 28, 2013: http://www.aacu.org/liberaleducation/le-fa12/bennett_cornwell_al-lail_schenck.cfm

Benyon, H. (1973). *Working for Ford*. Hammondsworth: Penguin.

Berger P. & Luchmann, T. (1967). *The social construction of reality*. New York: Anchor.

Bernstein, J. (1992). *The fate of art: Aesthetic alienation from Kant to Derrida and Adorno* Cambridge, UK: Polity Press.

Blake, P. (1996). *The master builders: Le Corbusier, Mies van der Rohe, Frank Lloyd Wright*. New York: W.W. Norton & Company.

Beynon, H. (1973). *Working for Ford*. London: Allen Lane, Penguin Books.

Bobbitt, F. (1918). *The curriculum*. Boston: Houghton Mifflin Co.

Bodrova, E., & Leong, D, (2007). *Tools of the mind: The Vygotskyan approach to early childhood education*. New York, NY: Pearson.

Bourdieu, P. (1993). *The field of cultural production*. New York, NY: Columbia University Press.

Bourdieu, P., & Passeron, J. (1977). *Reproduction in education, society and culture*. London: Sage Publications.

Bowers, C. A. (1980). Curriculum as Cultural Reproduction: An Examination of Metaphor as a Carrier of Ideology. *Teachers College Record*, 88(2), 267–289.

Boyles, D. (2012). Dewey, ecology, and education: historical and contemporary debates over Dewey's naturalism and (transactional) realism. *Educational Theory* 62(2), 143–161.

Burkes, B. (2001). Full moon: The imagery of wholeness and celebration. *NWSA Journal*, 13(2), 74–79.

Burns, J.M. (1978/1982). *Leadership*. New York: Harper.

Burris, C. (2013). Who are the 'enemies' of Common Core. *The Washington Post* (retrieved November 29, 2013 from http://www.washingtonpost.com)

Calhoun-Brown, A. (June 2000). Upon this rock: The Black Church, nonviolence, and the Civil Rights Movement. *Political Science and Politics*, 33(2),168–174.

Callejo Perez, D., Fain, S. M., & Slater, J. J. (Eds.). (2004). *Pedagogy of place: Seeing space as cultural education*. New York, NY: Peter Lang.

Carlson, D. L. (1982). An ontological grounding for curriculum. *Journal of Curriculum Theorizing*, 4 (Summer), 207–215.

Carson, C. (1986). Civil rights reform and the Black freedom struggle. In C. Eagles (Ed.). *The Civil Rights Movement in America*, p. 19–32. Jackson, MS: University Press of Mississippi.

Carson, C., Lapsansky-Werner, E. J., & Nash, B (2005). *African-American lives: The struggle for freedom*. New York: Pearson Longman.

Cary, L.J. (2006). *Curriculum spaces: Discourse, postmodernism, and educational research*. New York: Peter Lang.

Casemore, B. (2005). The language and politics of place: Autobiographical curriculum inquiry in the American South. Unpublished dissertation. Louisiana State University and Agricultural and Mechanical College. Baton Rouge, LA.

Castenell, L. & Pinar, W. (1993). *Curriculum as Racial Text*. Albany, NY: State University of New York Press.

Cissna, K. N., & Anderson, R. (1998). Theorizing about dialogic moments: The Buber-Rogers position and postmodern themes. *Communication Theory, 8*, 63–104.

Clottes, J.,& Lewis-Williams, D. (1998). *The Shamans of Prehistory: Trance and Magic in the Painted Caves*. New York: Harry N. Abrams.

Commager, H.S. (1950). *The American mind*. New Haven, CT: Yale University Press.

Common Core: State Standards Initiative (Retrieved November 29, 2013 from http://www.corestandards.org/)

Constantine, J., Player D., Silva, T., Hallgren, K., Grider, M., and Deke, J. (2009). *An evaluation of teachers trained through different routes to certification, final report* (NCEE 2009-4043). Washington, DC: National Center for Education Evaluation and Regional Assistance, Institute of Education Sciences, U.S. Department of Education.

Counts, G. (1932). *Dare the schools build a new social order?* New York: John Day Co.

Counts, G. (1971). *The American road to culture*. New York: Arno Press.

Cremin, L. (1961). *The transformation of the schools*. New York: Teachers College Press.

Cremin, L. (1980). *American education: The national experience*. New York: Harper Collins.

Culler, J. (1976/1979). *Structuralist poetics: Structuralism, linguistics, and the study of literature* Ithaca, NY: Cornell University Press.

Dahl, R.A. (1970). *After the revolution*. New Haven, CT: Yale University Press.

Darling-Hammond, L. (December 1999). *Teacher quality and student achievement: A review of state policy evidence*. Seattle, WA: University of Washington Center for the Study of Teaching and Policy.

Darling-Hammond, L., Berry, B. Thorenson, A. (2001). Does teacher education matter? Evaluating the evidence. *Educational evaluation and policy analysis, 23*(1), 57–77.

Dassbach, C.H.A. (1991). The origins of Fordism: The introduction of mass production and the five-dollar wage. *Critical Sociology, 18*, 77–90.

Delanty, G. (2006). The cosmopolitan imagination: Critical cosmopolitanism and social theory. *The British Journal of Sociology, 57*(1), 25–47.

Deleuze, G., & Guattari, F. (1996). *Qu'est-ce que la philosophie?* Paris: Les Editions de Minuit.

Derrida, J. (1978). *Writing and difference*. Chicago: University of Chicago Press.

Derrida, J. (1981). *Positions*. Chicago: University of Chicago Press.

Derrida, J. (1982) *Margins of philosophy*. A. Bass, trans. Chicago: University of Chicago Press.

Dewey, J. (1896). The reflex arc concept in psychology. *Psychological Review, 3*, 357–370.

Dewey, J. (1897). My pedagogic creed. *The School Journal,* 56(3), 77–80.

Dewey, J. (1910). *How we think.* New York: D.C. Heath.

Dewey, J. (1915/1944). *Democracy and education.* New York: The Free Press.

Dewey, J. (1916). *Democracy and education: An introduction to the philosophy of education.* New York: Macmillan.

Dewey, J. (1927). *The public and its problems.* New York: Swallow Press.

Dewey, J. (1929). *The sources of a science of education.* New York: Horace Liveright.

Dewey, J. (1929/1984). The quest for certainty: A study of the relation of knowledge and action. In J. A. Boydston (Ed.) *John Dewey: the later works, 1925–1953, Vol. 4:* 1929. Carbondale: Southern Illinois University Press.

Dewey, J. (1934a). *Art as experience.* New York: The Berkeley Publishing Group.

Dewey, J. (1934b). *A common faith.* New Haven: Yale University Press.

Dewey, J. (1938). *Experience and education.* New York: Collier Books.

Dewey, J. (1938/1991). Logic: The theory of inquiry. In J. A. Boydston (Ed.) *John Dewey: The Later Works, 1925–1953:* Vol. 12: 1938. Carbondale: Southern Illinois University Press.

Dewey, J. (1959). *Moral principles in education.* New York: Philosophical Library.

Dewey, J. (1994). *Experience and nature.* Chicago: Open Court Publishing Company.

Dewey, J. (1999). *The Essential Dewey* (2 volumes edited by Hickman, L., and Alexander, T.) Bloomington, IN: Indiana University Press.

Dews, P. (1987). *Logics of disintegration: Post-structuralist thought and the claims of critical theory.* London: Verso.

Dickie, G., Scalfini, R., & Roblin, R. (1989). *Aesthetics: A critical anthology.* New York: St. Martin's Press.

Dittmer, J. (1995). *Local people: The struggle for civil rights in Mississippi.* Urbana, IL: University of Illinois Press.

Douglass, F. (1986). *The narrative of Frederick Douglass.* New York: Penguin.

DuFour, R. & Eaker, R. (1998). *Professional learning communities at work: Best practices for enhancing student achievement.* Bloomington, IN: Solution Tree.

Durkheim, E. (2001). *The elementary forms of religious life.* C. Cosman (Trans.). New York: Oxford University Press.

Eagles, C. (2000). Toward new histories of the civil rights era. *Journal of Southern History,* 67 (4), 815–848.

Eagleton, T. (1983). *Literary theory: An introduction.* Oxford, England: Blackwell.

Eisner, E. (1979/2000). *The educational imagination: On the design and evaluation of school programs.* New York: Macmillan.

Eisner, E. (1998). *The enlightened eye: Qualitative inquiry and the enhancement of educational practice.* Upper Saddle River, NJ: Prentice Hall.

Ek, A. & Macintyre Latta, M. (2013). Preparing to teach: Redeeming the potentialities of the present through "conversations of practice." *Education and Culture,* 29(1), 84–104.

Euchner, C. (1994). *Extraordinary politics.* Boulder, CO: Westview.

Fisher, W. P. & Klein, M. F. (1978). Challenging simplistic beliefs about curriculum. *Educational Leadership,* 35(5), 390–393.

Foster, W. P. (2002). The decline of the local: A challenge to educational leadership. *Educational Administration Quarterly*, 4 (2), 176–191.

Foucault, M. (1967/1984). Of other spaces, Heterotopias. *Architecture, Mouvement, Continuité* 5, pp. 46–49. The publication of this text written in 1967 was auhtorized by Michel Foucault in 1984.

Foucault, M. (1977). *Language, counter-memory, practice: Selected essays and interviews*. Ithaca, NY: Cornell University Press.

Foucault, M. (1980). *Power/knowledge*. New York: Pantheon.

Freire, P. (1970/1997) *Pedagogy of the oppressed*. New York: Continuum.

Freire, P. (1995). *Pedagogy of hope: Reliving pedagogy of the oppressed*. New York: Continuum.

Fromm, E. (1941). *Escape from freedom*. New York: Holt.

Garrison, J. (1997). *Dewey and eros: Wisdom and desire in the art of teaching*. New York: Teachers College Press.

Geertz, C. (1973). *The interpretation of cultures*. New York: Basic Books.

Geertz, C. (1974). *Art as a cultural system*. New York: Basic Books.

Giddens, D. (1976). *New rules of sociological method*. London: Hutchinson.

Giddens, D. (1991). *Modernity and self-identity*. Palo Alto, CA: Stanford University Press.

Giroux, H. A. (1979). Toward a new sociology of curriculum. *Educational Leadership*, 37(3), 248–253.

Giroux, H. (1988). *Teachers as intellectuals*. Westport, CT: Praeger.

Glazer, N. (1997). *We are all multiculturalists now?* Cambridge, MA: Harvard University Press.

Goldstein, A. (2013). Massimiliano Gioni on his Venice Biennale, and "Trying to See More." *Artvoice*. Accessed, February 21, 2014: http://www.artspace.com/magazine/interviews_features/massimiliano_gioni_venice_biennale_interview

Greene, M. (1995). *Releasing the imagination: Essays on education, the arts, and social change*. San Francisco, CA: Jossey-Bass.

Greene, M. (1971). Curriculum and consciousness. *Teachers College Record*, 73(2), 253–270.

Greene, M. (2001). *Variations on a blue guitar*. New York: Teachers College Press.

Greene, M. (2004). *Releasing the imagination: Essays on education, the arts, and social change*. Washington, DC: National Association of Independent Schools.

Gupta, A. (1995). Blurred boundaries: The discourse of corruption, the culture of politics, and the imagined state. *American Ethnologist, 22*, 375–402.

Haacke, H. (1983). All the "art" that's fit to show. In A. A. Bronson & P. Gale (Eds.), *Museums by Artists* (pp. 151–152). Toronto: Art Metropole.

Habermas, J. (Summer 1990). Remarks on the discussion. *Theory, Culture and Society*, 7: 127–132.

Habermas, J. (1992). *Postmetaphysical thinking: Philosophical essays*. Cambridge, MA: The MIT Press.

Hackett Fischer, D. (1995). *Albion's seed*. London: Oxford University Press.

Hansen, D. (2008). Curriculum and the idea of a cosmopolitan inheritance, *Journal of Curriculum Studies*, 40(3), 289–312.

Hansen, D. (2009). Chasing butterflies without a net: Interpreting cosmopolitanism. *Study of Philosophy of Education*, Vol. 29, 151–166.

Hansen, D. (2010). Cosmopolitanism and education: A view from the ground. *Teachers College Record* 112(1), p. 1–30

Hansen, D. T., Burdick-Shepherd, S., Commarano, C., Obelleiro, G. (2009). Education, values, and valuing in cosmopolitan perspective. *Curriculum Inquiry*, 39(5), 587–612.

Heidegger, M. (1962). *Being and time*. Trans. by J. Macquarrie. New York: Harper & Row.

Helfenbein, R. (2004). A radical geography: Curriculum theory, performance, and landscape. *Journal of Curriculum Theorizing*, 20(3), 67–75.

Hinderliter, S. B., Kaizen, W., Maimon, V., Mansoor, J., & McCormick, S. (Eds.). (2009). *Communities of sense: Rethinking aesthetics and politics*. Durham, NC: Duke University Press.

Hoffer, E. (1951). *The true believer: Thoughts on mass movements*. New York: Harper & Row.

Hofstadter, R. (1963). *Anti-intellectualism in American life*. New York: Vintage.

Horkheimer, M. (1982). *Critical Theory*. New York: Seabury Press.

House of Representatives, *No Child Left Behind Act Rewards Progress, Corrects Failure, One Hundred and Seventh Congress, First Session, May, 16, 2001, 107th Cong. Washington: U.S. Government Printing Office, 2001, H2188.

House of Representatives, United States Congress., *The Obama Administration's Educational Agenda, Hearing Before the Committee on Education and Labor, One Hundred Eleventh Congress, First Session, May 20, 2009, 111th Cong. Washington, DC: U.S. Government Printing Office, 2009.

Howard, E. R. (1976). Can accountability improve secondary education? *Educational Leadership*, 33(8), 559–560.

Huebner, D. (1967). Curriculum as concern for man's temporality. *Theory into Practice*, 6(4), 172–179,

Huebner, D. (1975). Curricular language and classroom meanings. In W. Pinar (Ed.). *Curriculum theorizing: The Reconceptualists*, p. 217–236. Berkeley, CA: McCutchan.

Huebner, D. (1986). Curriculum as concern for man's temporality. *Theory into Practice*, Vol. 26, 324–331.

Huebner, D. (1999). Education and spirituality. I. V. Hillis (Ed.), *The lure of the transcendent: Collected essays by Dwayne E. Huebner*. Mahwah, NJ: Lawrence Erlbaum Associates, pp. 401–461.

Hunt, B. (1978). Who and what are to be evaluated? *Educational Leadership*, 35(4), 260–263.

Illich, I. (1971). *Deschooling society*. New York: Harper & Row.

Jackson, P. (1998). *John Dewey and the lessons of art*. New Haven, CT: Yale University Press.

Jennings, T. W. (1982). On ritual knowledge. *The Journal of Religion*, 62(2), 111–127.

Kaestle, C. (1983). *Pillars of the Republic: Common schools and American society, 1780–1860*. New York: Hill and Wang.

Karier, C. (1975). *Man, society and education*. Glenview, IL: Scott, Foresman.

Katz, M.B. (1968) *The irony of early school reform*. Cambridge, MA: Harvard University Press.

Katz, M. B. (2012). *Reconstructing American education*. Cambridge, MA: Harvard University Press.

Kellner, D. (2003). *Media spectacle*. New York: Psychology Press.

Kierkegaard, S. (1958). *Edifying discourses: A selection*. New York: Harper & Brothers.

Kincheloe, J. L. (1991). Willis Morris and the southern curriculum: Emancipating the southern ghosts. In Kincheloe, J.L. & Pinar, W. (Eds.). *Curriculum as social psychoanalysis: The significance of place.* Albany, NY: State University of New York Press.

Kincheloe, J. L. (1998). Pinar's Currere and identity in hyperreality: Grounding the post-formal notion of intrapersonal intelligence. In William F. Pinar (Ed.), *Curriculum: Toward New Identities* (pp. 129–142). New York: Routledge.

Kliebard, H. (1995). *The struggle for the American curriculum, 1893–1958.* Boston: Routledge.

Kohn, M., & Mithen, S. (1999). Handaxes: Products of sexual selection? *Antiquity—Oxford,* 73, 518–526.

Kreyling, M. (2001). *Inventing southern literature.* Jackson, MS: University of Mississippi Press.

Kunstler, H. J. (1994). *The Geography of Nowhere: The rises and decline of America's man-made landscape.* New York: Touchstone.

Lake, R. (2010). Reconstructing multicultural education: Transcending the essentialist/relativist dichotomy through personal story. *Multicultural Education,* 18(1), 43–47.

Lakoff, G. & Johnson, M. (1980). *Metaphors we live by.* Chicago, IL: The University of Chicago Press.

Langer, S. K. (1960). *Philosophy in a new key.* Cambridge: Harvard University Press.

Latta, M., (2001). *The possibilities of play in the classroom.* New York: Peter Lang.

Lawson, S. (1991). *Running for freedom: Civil Rights and Black politics in America since 1941.* Philadelphia, PA: Temple University Press.

Le Corbusier. (1967). *The radiant city: Elements of a doctrine of urbanism to be used as the basis of our machine-age civilization.* London: The Orion Press.

Leppert, R. (2004). The social discipline of listening. In J. Drobnick (Ed.), *Aural Cultures* (pp. 19–35). Toronto: YYZ Books.

Lipskey, W. E. (1976). The student as data source. *Educational Leadership,* 34(1), 17–20.

Lorde, A. (1972/1992). To my daughter, the junkie on the train. *Undersong: Chosen poems old and new* (Revised). New York: W. W. Norton & Company.

Lyotard, J. (1984). *The postmodern condition.* Minneapolis, MN: University of Minnesota Press.

Marrett, R. R. (1914). *The threshold of religion.* London: Methuen.

Marshall, D. (2002). Behavior, belonging, and belief: A theory of ritual practice. *Sociological Theory,* 20(3), 360–380.

Matustik, M. & Westphal, M. (1995) *Kierkegaard in post/modernity.* Bloomington, IN: Indiana University Press.

Means, A. J. (2010). Aesthetics, affect, and educational politics. *Educational Philosophy and Theory,* doi: 10.111/j.1469-5812.2009.00615.x

Means, A. J. (2014). Beyond the poverty of national security: Toward a critical human security perspective in educational policy. *Journal of Education Policy,* 29(1), 1–23.

Mehaffy, M. W. and Salingaros, N. A. (2013). A vision for architecture as more than the sum of its parts. *On the Commons.* Posted November 11, 2013. Retrieved December 17, 2013 from http://onthecommons.org/magazine/vision-architecture-more-sum-its-parts.

Menand, L. (2000). *The metaphysical club.* New York: Farrar, Straus and Giroux.

Milligan, J. (2001). Multiculturalism and the idolatry of inclusion, in S. Steinberg (Ed.). *Multi/Intercultural Conversations.* New York: Peter Lang.

Molnar, A. (1996). *Giving kids the business: The commercialization of America's schools*. Boulder, CO: Westview Press.

Moran, P. W. (2012). Efficiency, standardization and mitigating risk: The strange career of scientific management in American education, 1890–2010. In S. Bialostok and R.L. Whitman (Eds.), *Education and the risk society: Theories, discourse and risk identities in education contexts* (pp. 55–74). Rotterdam, NE: Sense Publishers.

Morgan, E. (1975). *American slavery, American freedom: The ordeal of colonial Virginia*. New York: Norton.

Morris, W. (1971). *Yazoo: Integration in a deep-Southern town*. New York: Harper's Magazine Press.

Murphy, B. (2005). Memory, history and museums. *Museum, 57*, 70–78.

Nancy, J-L. (2001). *La pensée-dérobée*. Paris: Galilé.

Nancy, J-L. (2002). *La création du monde ou la mondialisation*. Paris: Galilé.

National Center for Educational Statistics. *Digest of Educational Statistics*. Retrieved November 15, 2013 from http://www.nces.ed.gov/programs/digest

Nehamas, A. (1987). *The art of living: Socratic reflections from Plato to Foucault*. Berkeley, CA: University of California Press.

New York State Common Core Mathematics Curriculum http://www.engageny.org/sites/default/files/resource/attachments/algebra-i-m1-teacher-materials.pdf

Nowell, A., & Chang, M. L. (1997/2009). The case against sexual selection as an explanation of handaxe morphology. *Paleoanthropology, 77–99*.

Nussbaum, M. C. (2009). *Cultivating humanity: A classical defense of reform in liberal education*. Cambridge, MA: Harvard University Press.

Onuf, N. (1989). *World of our making*. Columbia, SC: University of South Carolina Press.

Passerin d'Entreves, M. (1993). *The political philosophy of Hannah Arendt*. London: Routledge.

Petrunic, A. M. (2005). No Man's Land: The intersection of Balkan space and identity. *History of Intellectual Culture, 5*(1), 1–10.

Pharr, S. (1996). *In the time of the right: Reflections on liberation*. Oakland, CA: Chardon Press.

Peirce, C. S. (1999). *The essential Peirce*. Bloomington, IN: Indiana University Press.

Piery, L. (2001). *Art Brut: The origins of outsider art*. Paris: Flammarion Press.

Pinar, W. F. (2001). *The gender of racial politics and violence in America: Lynching, prison rape, and the crisis of masculinity*. New York: Peter Lang.

Pinar, W. F. (2004). *What Is curriculum theory?* Mahwah, NJ: Lawrence Erlbaum.

Pinar, W. F. (2006). *The synoptic text today and other essays: Curriculum development after the Reconceptualists*. New York: Peter Lang.

Pinar, William F. (2008). *What is curriculum theory?* Taylor & Francis e-Library.

Pinar, W. (2009). *The worldliness of a cosmopolitan education: Passionate lives in public service*. New York: Routledge.

Pinar, W. (2011). *What is curriculum theory?* New York: Routledge.

Pinar, W. (2012). *What is curriculum theory, 2nd Edition*. New York, NY: Routledge.

Pinkard, T. (1994). *Hegel's phenomenology: The sociality of creation*. New York: Cambridge University Press.

Programme for International Student Assessment. Organization for Economic Co-operation and Development. Retrieved October 31, 2013 from http://www.oecd.org/pisa

Popper, K. (1972). *Objective knowledge: An evolutionary approach*. London: Oxford University Press.

Popper, K. (1984/1992). *In search of a better world: Lectures and essays from thirty years*. New York: Routledge.

Postman, N. (1995). *The end of education: Redefining the value of school*. New York: Alfred A. Knopf.

Prosser, C. (1916). *Study of the Boston Mechanic Arts High School; being a report to the Boston School Committee*. Columbia University Thesis.

Purpel, D. & McLaurin, W. (2004). *Reflections on the moral and spiritual crisis in education*. New York: Peter Lang.

Rader, M. (1979). *A modern book of esthetics* (5th edition). New York: Harcourt College Publishers.

Rancière, J. (2002). The aesthetic revolution and its outcomes. *New Left Review, 14*, 133–151.

Rancière, J. (2008). Aesthetic separation, aesthetic community: Scenes from the aesthetic regime of art. *Art and Research: A Journal of Ideas, Contexts and Methods 2*(1), retrieved October 31, 2013 http://www.artandresearch.org.uk/v2n1/ranciere.html

Rancière, R. (2010). *Dissensus: On politics and aesthetics*. London: Continuum.

Ravitch, D. (1983). *The troubled crusade: American education, 1945–1980*. New York: Basic Books.

Reynolds, W. (2013). *A curriculum of place: Understandings emerging through the Southern mist*. New York: Peter Lang.

Richter, P. E. (1967). *Perspectives in Aesthetics: Plato to Camus*. New York: Odyssey Press.

Rickover, H. G. (1959). *Education and freedom*. New York: E. P. Dutton & Co.

Rickover, H. G. (1963). *American education: A national failure*. New York: E. P. Dutton & Co.

Ricoeur, P. (1975). *The rule of metaphor: Multi-disciplinary studies in the creation of meaning in language* (trans. Robert Czerny with Kathleen McLaughlin and John Costello). London: Routledge and Kegan Paul 1978.

Rodin, J., & Steinberg, S. P., (Eds.). (2011). *Public discourse in America: Conversation and community in the twenty-first century*. Philadelphia: University of Pennsylvania Press.

Rodriguez, C., & Trueba, E. T. (1998). Leadership, education, and political action: The emergence of new Latino ethnic identities. In Yali Zou & Enrique Treuba (Eds.), *Ethnic and identity power: Cultural contexts of political action in school and society* (pp. 42–66). Albany, NY: State University of New York Press.

Rorty, R. (1979). *Philosophy and the mirror of nature*. Princeton, NJ: Princeton University Press.

Rorty, R. (1982). *Consequences of pragmatism*. Minneapolis, MN: University of Minnesota Press.

Ross, M. (1984). *Aesthetic impulse*. New York: Elsevier Publishers.

Ruciman, W. C. (1978) *Max Weber: Selections in translation*. Cambridge, England: Cambridge University Press.

Rud, A. G. & Garrison, J. (2013). *Teaching with reverence: Reviving an ancient virtue for today's schools*. New York: Palgrave Macmillan.

Sabel, C. (1973). *Work and Politics*. Cambridge, England: Cambridge University Press.

Scheffler, I. (1997). *Symbolic worlds: Art, science, language, ritual*. New York: Cambridge University Press.

Schoolman, M. (2001). *Reason and horror: Critical theory, democracy, and aesthetic individuality*. New York: Routledge.

Schubert, W. H. (2009). *Love, justice, and education: John Dewey and the Utopians*. Charlotte: Information Age Publishing.

Schwab, J. J. (1969). The practical: A language for curriculum. *The School Review, 78*, 1–23.

Sennett, R. (1994). *Flesh and stone: The body and the city in western civilization*. New York: W. W. Norton & Company.

Sennett, R. (2004). *Respect in a world of inequality*. New York: W. W. Norton & Company.

Shapiro, L. (1980). The concept of ideology as evolved by Marx and adapted by Lenin. In M. Cranston (Ed.), *Ideology and politics*. The Hague, Netherlands: Walter de Gruyter.

Shapiro, N. S. & Levine, J. H. (1999). *Creating learning communities*. San Francisco: Jossey-Bass.

Slater, J.J., Callejo Perez, D.M., & Fain, S. (Eds.) (1998). *The war against the professions: The impact of politics and economics on the idea of the university*. Rotterdam: Sense Publishers.

Slattery, P. (1995). *Curriculum development in the postmodern era*. New York: Garland Publishing.

Smart, B. (1993). *Postmodernism*. New York: Routledge.

Soja, E. (1971). *The political organization of space*. Washington, DC: Association of American Geographers, Commission on College Geography.

Soja, E. (1989). *Postmodern geographies: The reassertion of space in critical social theory*. New York: Verso.

Sowell, T. (1981). *Ethnic America: A history*. New York: Basic Books.

Spring, J. (2005a). *The American school 1642–2004*. (6th ed.). Columbus, OH: McGraw-Hill.

Spring, J. (2005b). *Conflict of interests: The politics of American education*. (5th ed.). Columbus, OH: McGraw-Hill.

Sturrock, J. (1979). *Structuralism and Since: From Levi-Strauss to Derrida*. New York: Oxford University Press.

Talbert, S. & Boyles, D. (2005). Reconsidering learning communities: Expanding the discourse by challenging the discourse. *The Journal of General Education, 54*(3), 209–236.

Tanke, J. J. (2011). What is the aesthetic regime? *Parrhesia, 12*, 71–71.

Taylor, B. P. (2010). *Horace Mann's troubling legacy: The education of democratic citizens*. Lawrence, KS: University of Kansas Press.

Taylor, M. C. (1992). *Disfiguring: Art, architecture, religion*. Chicago: University of Chicago Press.

Tierney, W. G., & Lincoln, Y. S. (Eds.). (1997). *Representation and the text: Re-framing the narrative voice*. Albany, NY: State University of New York Press.

Tindall, G.B. (1964). Mythology: A new frontier in Southern history. In F. Vandiver (Ed.), *The idea of the South: Pursuit of a central theme*, pp. 1S16. Chicago: University of Chicago Press.

Turner, F.J. (1899). *The frontier in American history*. New York: Holt, Rinehart & Winston.

Tyack, D. (1974). *The one best system*. New York: Harcourt/Brace.

Tyler, L. L. (1978). Curriculum evaluation and persons. *Educational Leadership, 35*(4), 275–279.

Tyler, R. (1949). *Basic principles of curriculum*. Chicago: University of Chicago Press.

U.S. Department of Commerce, Census Bureau. Accessed October 31, 2013: http://www.census.gov.

U.S. Government Accountability Office, Teacher preparation: Multiple federal education offices support teacher preparation for instructing students with disabilities and English language learners, but systematic department wide coordination could enhance this assistance, in *Report to the Chairman, Subcommittee on Higher Education, Lifelong Learning, and Competitiveness, Committee on Education and Labor, House of Representatives*. Washington, DC: GAO, July 2009.

Vincent, G. (1900). *The social mind and education*. New York: Macmillan.

Vygotsky, L. (1967). Play and its role in the mental development of the child. *Soviet Psychology* 5(3), 6–18. (Original work published 1966).

Vygotsky, L. S. (1978). *Mind in society: The development of higher psychological processes*. Cambridge, MA: Harvard University Press.

Weber, C. (2005). Not without my sister(s): Imagining a moral America in Kandahar. *International Feminist Journal of Politics*, 7(3), 358–376.

White, W. (2010). Toward curricular coherence. *SUNY Faculty Bulletin*, Fall 2010, 7–8.

Wiggin, L. (1962). *Education and nationalism*. New York: Teachers College Press.

Williams, E. (1964/1966). *Capitalism and slavery*. London: Andre Deutsch.

Winston, A. A. & G. C. Cupchick (1992). The evaluation of high art and popular art by naïve and experienced viewers. *Visual Arts Research*, 18(1), 1–14.

Woodward, C.V. (1993). *The burden of Southern history*. Baton Rouge: University of Louisiana Press.